Headway

Academic Skills

Listening, Speaking, and Study Skills

INTRODUCTORY LEVEL Student's Book

Sarah Philpot and Lesley Curnick
Series Editors: Liz and John Soars

OXFORD

CONTENTS

1 A new start

LISTENING Nice to meet you

1 Work with a partner. Look at the pictures. Answer the questions.
  1 Where are the people?
  2 Who are the people?

2 `Read STUDY SKILL` Look at the badges.
  1 What information do you need for Badge 1?
  2 What information do you need for Badge 2?

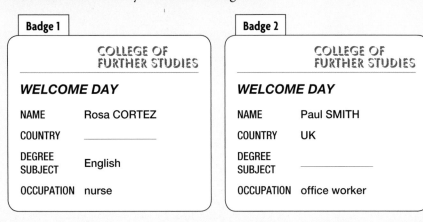

Badge 1		
COLLEGE OF FURTHER STUDIES		
WELCOME DAY		
NAME	Rosa CORTEZ	
COUNTRY	_____	
DEGREE SUBJECT	English	
OCCUPATION	nurse	

Badge 2		
COLLEGE OF FURTHER STUDIES		
WELCOME DAY		
NAME	Paul SMITH	
COUNTRY	UK	
DEGREE SUBJECT	_____	
OCCUPATION	office worker	

> **STUDY SKILL** Why listen?
>
> Think about the information you need **before** you listen. This helps you understand. For example:
> - Do you only need the general idea?
> - Do you need a piece of information, e.g. a name, a place, a subject?

3 🔊 1.1 Listen to Rosa and Paul. Complete the badges.

4 🎵 1.2 Read the rules. Use contractions or full forms to complete the questions. Listen and check your answers.

1 What _____ your name?
2 How _____ you?
3 Where _____ you from?
4 What _____ you _____ ?
5 What _____ your degree subject?

RULES Present Simple (1) *Wh-* questions		
With the verb *be* use a question word + *is / are*.		
What	*'s / is*	your name?
How	*'re / are*	you?
Where	*'s / is*	he / she from?
With other verbs, use a question word + *do / does* … + verb.		
Where	*do*	you teach?
What	*does*	he / she teach?
How many classes	*do*	they have?

5 Read STUDY SKILL 🎵 1.3 Listen to three conversations with the college receptionist. Complete the badges. Check your answers with a partner.

STUDY SKILL Listening for detail
When you listen for detail, e.g. for a name, a country, a number:
■ listen only for the information which you need.
■ do not try to understand everything.

Conversation 1

COLLEGE OF
FURTHER STUDIES

WELCOME DAY

NAME _____ WEBER

COUNTRY Germany

DEGREE SUBJECT history

OCCUPATION teacher

Conversation 2

COLLEGE OF
FURTHER STUDIES

WELCOME DAY

NAME Turan ERDEM

COUNTRY _____

DEGREE SUBJECT business management

OCCUPATION police officer

Conversation 3

COLLEGE OF
FURTHER STUDIES

WELCOME DAY

NAME Noor AL MANSOORI

COUNTRY UAE

DEGREE SUBJECT _____

OCCUPATION secretary

6 🎵 1.3 Listen to the conversations again. Tick (✓) the questions you hear.

1 ☐ What's your name?
2 ☐ How are you?
3 ☐ What's your degree subject?
4 ☐ Where are you from?
5 ☐ What do you do?

KEY LANGUAGE The alphabet

1 **Read STUDY SKILL** 💿 1.5 Listen and repeat the letters of the alphabet.

The alphabet

a b c d e f g h i j k l m
n o p q r s t u v w x y z

STUDY SKILL The alphabet

You need to know the alphabet:

- to understand how a word is spelled. Ask:
  How do you spell that? or *Could you spell that, please?*
- to give information, e.g. your name. Say:
  My name's Thomas, that's T-H-O-M-A-S.

💿 1.4 Listen.

2 💿 1.6 Work with a partner. Put the letters of the alphabet under the correct sound. Listen and check your answers.

/eɪ/	/iː/	/e/	/aɪ/	/əʊ/	/uː/	/ɑː/
say	be	egg	my	no	you	car
a	b					

3 💿 1.7 Listen and write the letters.

1 a ___ i ___ u
2 m ___ f ___ s
3 c ___ t ___ v
4 j ___ d ___ z
5 t ___ l ___ n

4 Work with a partner. Student A, look at page 73. Student B, look at page 76.

5 Answer the questions. Write the answer.

1 What's your favourite drink? _____
2 What's the make of your car? _____
3 What's the make of your phone? _____
4 What's your favourite food? _____
5 Who's your best friend? _____

6 Work with a partner. Ask and answer the questions in exercise 5. Write your partner's answers. Ask for help with spelling.

1 _____
2 _____
3 _____
4 _____
5 _____

SPEAKING Good morning!

1 🔘 1.8 Listen and repeat the questions.

   1 What's your name?
   2 Where are you from?
   3 What course are you on?
   4 What do you do?

2 Work with a partner. Ask and answer
the questions in exercise 1.

3 Read STUDY SKILL 🔘 1.9 Listen and complete the conversations.

Conversation 1
A What's your _____?
B My name's Alan Waters.
A Sorry, could you _____ that _____, please?
B Alan, Alan Waters.

Conversation 2
A Where's Noor _____?
B The UAE.
A _____?
B The UAE.

> **STUDY SKILL** Asking for help (1)
>
> If you don't understand, ask:
> *Sorry, could you repeat that, please?*
> *I'm sorry, could you say that again?*
> *Sorry?*

4 Work with a partner. Student A, look at page 73. Student B, look at page 76.

5 🔘 1.10 Listen and repeat the greetings and replies.

> **LANGUAGE BANK** Greetings and replies
>
> | **Greeting people** | **Replying** |
> | --- | --- |
> | *Good morning!* | *Good morning!* |
> | *Good afternoon!* | *Good afternoon!* |
> | *Good evening!* | *Good evening!* |
> | *Hello! / Hi!* | *Hello! / Hi!* |
> | *Goodbye! / Bye!* | *Goodbye! / Bye!* |
> | *Nice to meet you.* | *Nice to meet you, too.* |
> | *How are you?* | *Fine, thanks. And you?* |
> | *See you later.* | *See you later.* |
> | *See you tomorrow.* | *Yes, see you tomorrow.* |

6 🔘 1.11 Listen and reply. Use phrases from the Language Bank.

7 Work with a partner. Take turns to greet and reply. Use the
phrases from the Language Bank.

   A *How are you?*
   B *Fine, thanks. And you?*

   A *Good evening!*
   B *Good evening!*

VOCABULARY DEVELOPMENT Classroom instructions

1 Read STUDY SKILL Match an instruction from the box with a picture or example. Compare your answers with your partner.

> ask and answer   circle   ~~complete~~   listen to   look at
> match   repeat   tick   underline   work with a partner

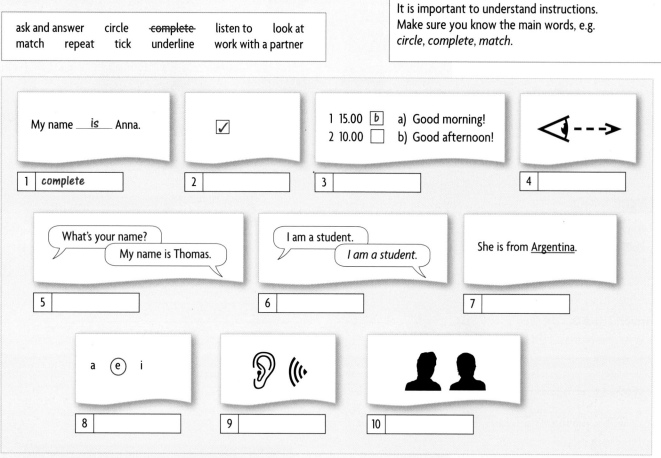

1	complete
2	
3	
4	
5	
6	
7	
8	
9	
10	

2 🔊 1.12 Listen and follow the instructions.

> **1** morning   afternoon   evening
> **2** 1 ☐ 11 a.m.   a) Good afternoon!
>   2 ☐ 3 p.m.   b) Good evening!
>   3 ☐ 7 p.m.   c) Good morning!
> **3** g   h   i   j   k
> **4** 10 ☐   11 ☐   12 ☐   13 ☐
> **5** Ahmed _____ from Oman.

3 Read STUDY SKILL Work with a partner. What do you say?
1 Ask for the meaning of *easy*.
2 Ask for the pronunciation of *easy*.
3 Ask for a translation of *easy*.
4 Ask the teacher to speak more slowly.

REVIEW

1 Work with a partner. Look at the notice. Answer the questions.
  1 What are the classes?
  2 When does enrolment begin?

2 Work with a partner. Look at the enrolment form. Tick (✓) the questions the secretary needs to ask.
  1 ☐ What's your name?
  2 ☐ How old are you?
  3 ☐ What do you do?
  4 ☐ Where are you from?
  5 ☐ What course are you on?
  6 ☐ What's your level of English?

The Oxford Summer School

English conversation classes

Conversation classes for university students from beginner to advanced.

Enrolment for classes begins on Monday 4th October.

Please bring ID to enrol.

The Oxford Summer School

ENROLMENT FORM

English conversation classes

Name: Susanne
Country: _____
Course: _____

English language level: ☐ Beginner
                         ☐ Elementary
                         ☐ Pre-Intermediate
                         ☐ Intermediate
                         ☐ Upper-Intermediate
                         ☐ Advanced

3 🔊 1.14 Listen to the conversation. Check your answers to exercise 2.

4 🔊 1.14 Listen again and complete the enrolment form for Susanne.

5 Work with a partner. Take turns to be the secretary and the student. Have a conversation and complete the enrolment form for your partner. Remember to:
  • greet your partner.
  • ask questions.
  • ask for help with spelling.

The Oxford Summer School

ENROLMENT FORM

English conversation classes

Name: _____
Country: _____
Course: _____

English language level: ☐ Beginner
                         ☐ Elementary
                         ☐ Pre-Intermediate
                         ☐ Intermediate
                         ☐ Upper-Intermediate
                         ☐ Advanced

2 Tourism

LISTENING SKILLS Predicting • Hearing sentences
KEY LANGUAGE Understanding numbers (1) and (2)
SPEAKING SKILLS Presentations • Helping the listener (1)
VOCABULARY DEVELOPMENT Using a dictionary (1)

LISTENING Weather

1 Work with a partner. Match a picture with a word or words in the box.

dry	rain	rainy	~~sun~~	sunny	wet	wind	windy
cold	cool	hot	warm				

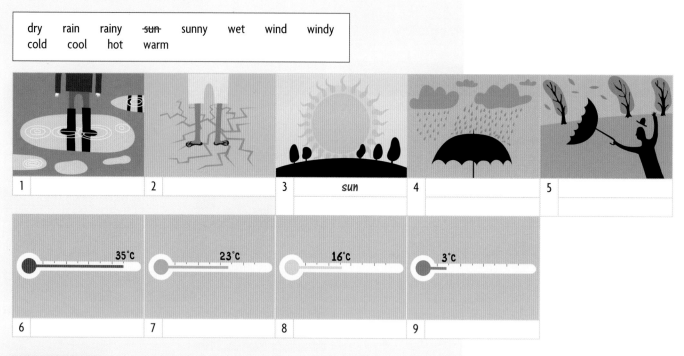

| 1 | 2 | 3 sun | 4 | 5 |

| 6 35°c | 7 23°c | 8 16°c | 9 3°c |

2 **Read STUDY SKILL** Look at CITY FILE 1. What is the lecture about?

a) geography b) agriculture c) climate

STUDY SKILL Predicting

Before you listen to a presentation, think about the information you will hear. Look at the slides.
- Use the title.
- Look at any pictures and slides.
- Think about important words on the topic.

This helps you understand the presentation.

3 Work with a partner. Look at 1–3 in CITY FILE 1. Is the missing information a word (W) or a number (N)?

1 ___   2 ___   3 ___

4 🔘 2.1 Listen and complete CITY FILE 1. Check your answers with a partner.

CITY FILE 1 Weather around the world

Place	Mexico City
Month	June
Climate	warm and ^{1}_____
Temperature	^{2}_____ . ___°C
Hours of sun a day	^{3}_____

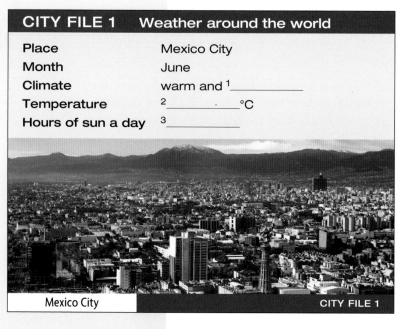

Mexico City   CITY FILE 1

5 Look at CITY FILE 2. Answer the questions.

a) What is the country?
b) How many hours of sun a day are there?
c) What information do you need for 1–3?

6 🎧 2.2 Listen to a student talk. Complete CITY FILE 2. Check your answers with a partner.

CITY FILE 2	Weather around the world
Place	Singapore
Month	1_____
Climate	2_____ and rainy
Temperature	3_____°C
Hours of sun a day	6

Singapore   CITY FILE 2

7 🎧 2.3 Listen and read the sentences. What happens at the end of the first sentence? **Read STUDY SKILL**

Let's look at Mexico City. In June, the climate is warm and dry.

STUDY SKILL Hearing sentences

In **written English**, there is a full stop at the end of a sentence.

In **spoken English**, there is a short pause at the end of a sentence.

Hearing the short pause helps you understand.

8 Work with a partner. Add a full stop at the end of the five sentences in the text. Put a capital letter at the beginning of each sentence.

good morning, my name is Diana I come from Malta my talk is about the weather in my country in June, it is hot and dry the temperature is 28°C, and there are about eleven hours of sun a day

9 🎧 2.4 Listen and check your answers.

Malta

KEY LANGUAGE Numbers 1–100

1 🔊 2.5 Listen and repeat the numbers.

1	2	3	4	5	6	7	8	9	10
11	12	13	14	15	16	17	18	19	20

2 🔊 2.6 Listen and write the missing numbers. Check your answers with a partner.

a) 5   7   ___   20
b) 4   ___   14   17
c) 1   3   6   ___
d) 2   10   ___   18

3 🔊 2.7 Write the numbers you hear. Check your answers with a partner.

a) **50**   f) ___
b) ___   g) ___
c) ___   h) ___
d) ___   i) ___
e) ___

4 `Read STUDY SKILL` 🔊 2.9 Listen and underline the number you hear. Check your answers with a partner.

a) 14   40
b) 15   50
c) 16   60
d) 17   70
e) 18   80
f) 19   90

STUDY SKILL Understanding numbers (1)

Some numbers sound similar, e.g. *13* and *30*.

Listen for the word stress. This helps you understand which number it is.

thirteen   *thirty*
fourteen   *forty*

🔊 2.8 Listen.

5 `Read STUDY SKILL` 🔊 2.10 Listen and complete the sentences with a number.

1 In London in June, the temperature is about _____°C.
2 There are about _____ hours of sun a day.
3 The class starts at _____ o'clock.
4 I'm _____ years old.
5 There are _____ students in my class.

STUDY SKILL Understanding numbers (2)

Numbers are used to give information, e.g. about temperature, age, time.

The temperature is 39°C.
I am 18 years old.
The library opens at 9 o'clock.

It is important to understand and say numbers correctly.

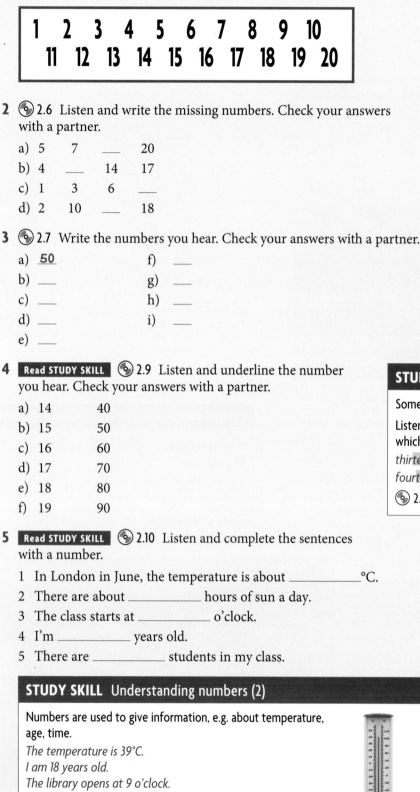

6 Work with a partner. Student A, look at page 73. Student B, look at page 76.

SPEAKING Places

1 **Read STUDY SKILL** 🔊 2.11 Listen to the start of two presentations. Is presentation 1 or presentation 2 better?

2 Work with a partner. Is expression a) or expression b) better for a presentation? Why?

1 a) Hello.
  b) Good afternoon.
2 a) My name is …
  b) I'm …
3 a) My talk is about …
  b) Here's my talk.
4 a) Thanks.
  b) Thank you for listening.

| STUDY SKILL Presentations |

> **STUDY SKILL Presentations**
>
> It is important to start and end a presentation clearly.
>
> - Greet the listeners, and say your name:
>   *Good morning / afternoon. My name is Yuko.*
> - Say the topic of your talk:
>   *My talk is about tourism in Tokyo.*
> - Say thank you at the end:
>   *Thank you for listening.*

3 Add the headings in the box to CITY FILE 3.

> Place
> Famous for
> Number of tourists
> Population

CITY FILE 3   Topic: Tourism in New York

a) _____ New York, USA
b) _____ about 8 million
c) _____ the Empire State Building
                         the Statue of Liberty
d) _____ about 50 million per year

Empire State Building   Statue of Liberty   CITY FILE 3

4 Use the notes in CITY FILE 3 to complete the text. Check your answers with a partner.

> 1_____ is a large city in the USA.
> It has a population of about 2_____
> million people. It is famous for the
> 3_____ and the
> 4_____ of 5_____. About
> 6_____ million tourists visit New
> York each 7_____.

5 **Read STUDY SKILL** Work with a partner. Give a talk using the text in exercise 4.

- Remember to say *Good morning* or *Good afternoon*, your name, and the topic.
- Give the talk.
- Thank your listeners.

> **STUDY SKILL Helping the listener (1)**
>
> Help your listeners understand your talk.
>
> - Speak slowly and clearly.
> - Make a short pause at the end of sentences.
> - Say important information clearly, e.g. numbers.

6 Work with a partner. Student A, look at page 73. Student B, look at page 76.

7 Answer the questions about your partner's talk.

1 Did your partner speak clearly?
2 Did your partner make a short pause at the end of sentences?
3 Did your partner say numbers clearly?

VOCABULARY DEVELOPMENT Word stress

1 **Read STUDY SKILL** Work with a partner. How many syllables are there in each word?

1 rai|ny
2 degree
3 understand
4 Singapore
5 climate
6 eleven

2 🔊 2.13 Listen to the words in exercise 1. Underline the stressed syllable.

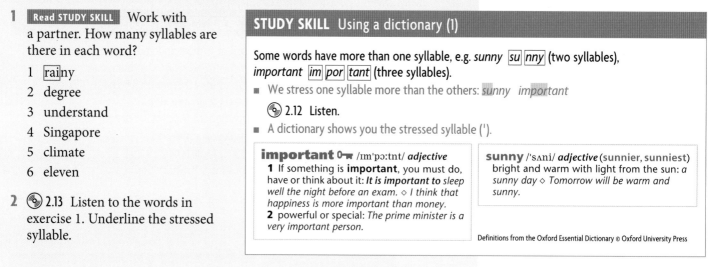

STUDY SKILL Using a dictionary (1)

Some words have more than one syllable, e.g. *sunny* su|nny (two syllables), *important* im|por|tant (three syllables).

■ We stress one syllable more than the others: *sunny* *important*

🔊 2.12 Listen.

■ A dictionary shows you the stressed syllable (').

important ⚬ /ɪmˈpɔːtnt/ *adjective*
1 If something is **important**, you must do, have or think about it: *It is important to sleep well the night before an exam.* ◇ *I think that happiness is more important than money.*
2 powerful or special: *The prime minister is a very important person.*

sunny /ˈsʌni/ *adjective* (sunnier, sunniest) bright and warm with light from the sun: *a sunny day* ◇ *Tomorrow will be warm and sunny.*

Definitions from the Oxford Essential Dictionary © Oxford University Press

3 Work with a partner. Say the words in the box. Put them under the correct heading.

adjective	afternoon	complete	number
sixteen	student	syllable	tourist	weather

two syllables	three syllables
	a̱djective

4 🔊 2.14 Listen to the words in exercise 3. Underline the stressed syllable.

5 Use a dictionary to check your answers.

6 Work with a partner. Look at the words. Answer the questions. Check your answers in a dictionary.

a) How many syllables are there?
b) Which syllable is stressed? Underline the stressed syllable.

1 unders̱tand ___3___
2 predict ___
3 morning ___
4 agriculture ___
5 eighteen ___
6 partner ___
7 thirty ___

7 🔊 2.15 Listen and check your answers.

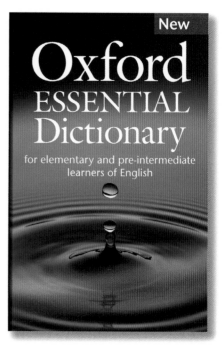

New

Oxford
ESSENTIAL
Dictionary

for elementary and pre-intermediate learners of English

REVIEW

1 🎧 2.16 Listen to the sentences about Rome. Count the number of sentences you hear, and write 1, 2, or 3.

a) —

b) —

c) —

The Coliseum, Rome

2 Work with a partner. Look at the pictures and the notes in CITY FILE 6. Predict the topic of the talk.

3 Work with a partner. For gaps 1–6 in CITY FILE 6, do you need a word (W) or a number (N)?

1 **W**

2 —

3 —

4 —

5 —

6 —

4 🎧 2.17 Listen to the talk and complete CITY FILE 6. Compare your answers with a partner.

CITY FILE 6	Topic: ¹_____, capital city of the Philippines
Population	about 11 million
Famous for	Malacanang Palace and Rizal ²_____
Number of tourists	³_____ per year
Best month to visit	⁴_____
Weather and temperature	warm and ⁵_____, ⁶_____°C

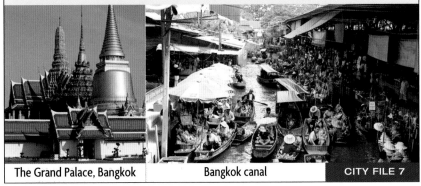

Malacanang Palace   Rizal Park, Manila   CITY FILE 6

5 Use the information in CITY FILE 7 to prepare a talk about Bangkok.

6 Work with a partner. Take turns to give the talk. Answer the questions about your partner.

Did your partner:

1 say *Good morning* or *Good afternoon*?

2 say his / her name and the topic?

3 speak clearly?

4 make a short pause at the end of sentences?

5 say numbers clearly?

6 say *Thank you* at the end of the talk?

CITY FILE 7	Topic: Bangkok, capital city of Thailand
Population	about 7 million
Famous for	canals, palaces, and markets
Number of tourists	about 7 million per year
Best month to visit	December
Weather and temperature	cool and dry, about 30°C

The Grand Palace, Bangkok   Bangkok canal   CITY FILE 7

3 Your day

LISTENING SKILLS Listening for the general idea
KEY LANGUAGE Telling the time • Time expressions
SPEAKING SKILLS Speaking politely
VOCABULARY DEVELOPMENT Recording vocabulary (1) and (2)

LISTENING Free time

1 ◎ 3.1 Work with a partner. Write the phrases in the box under the photos. Listen and repeat the phrases.

travel by bus	use a computer
visit famous places	watch television

2 **Read STUDY SKILL** ◎ 3.2 Listen to Julian. Which sentence gives the general idea?

1 ☐ Julian talks about his computer.
2 ☐ Julian talks about his studies.
3 ☐ Julian talks about his free time.

STUDY SKILL Listening for the general idea

When you listen for the general idea, do not try to understand every word. Listen for the main points.

3 ◎ 3.2 Listen again and tick (✓) the true sentences.

1 ☐ Julian visits famous places.
2 ☐ He travels by taxi.
3 ☐ He goes shopping.
4 ☐ He watches television.
5 ☐ He talks to his friends on the Internet.
6 ☐ He goes on Facebook.

4 Work with a partner. Look at the timetable. Answer the questions.

1 What day of the week is it?
2 When is the chemistry lecture?

5 ◎ 3.3 Listen to the telephone conversation. Answer the questions.

1 Who is talking?
   a) two teachers   b) two students
2 Who has the new timetable for Mondays?
   a) Paul   b) Ahmed

6 ◎ 3.3 Listen again. Complete the timetable with the words in the box. Compare your answers with a partner.

biology	~~chemistry~~	English	maths

Lecture timetable

MONDAY	Time	Lectures
morning	9.00	¹ _chemistry_
	11.00	² _____
afternoon	2.00	³ _____
	4.00	⁴ _____
TUESDAY	Time	Lectures

KEY LANGUAGE Time

1 ⊙ 3.4 Read the rules. Listen and match a time in the box with a picture.

| one forty-five | 8.00 | nine thirty | 4.40 |
| two fifty | 7.55 | eleven fifteen | 6.25 |

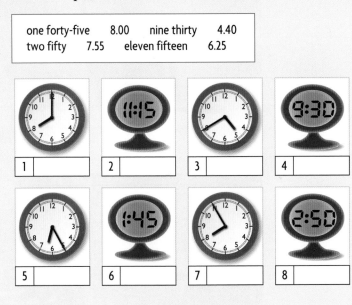

RULES Telling the time

Say the hour and then the minutes.
It's eight thirty (8.30).
It's ten forty-five (10.45).

For the part of day, say:
in the morning (00.00–12.00)
in the afternoon (12.00–6.00)
in the evening (6.00–12.00)

2 ⊙ 3.4 Listen again and repeat the times.

3 Work with a partner. Ask and say the times in the pictures.

A What's the time?
B It's two fifty.
A Thank you.

4 Work with a partner. Student A, look at page 74. Student B, look at page 77.

5 ⊙ 3.5 Read the rules. Work with a partner. Complete the text with *in*, *on*, or *at*. Listen and check your answers.

RULES Time expressions

Use a preposition with a time expression.
- Use **in** for a part of the day:
  in the morning(s)
- Use **at** for a time, and for **at** the weekend / **at** weekends:
  She gets up at 7.30.
  They play football at weekends.
- Use **on** for a day, and a part of the day:
  on Tuesday(s)
  on Tuesday afternoon(s)

Fatima is a business studies student. [1]_____ Mondays, she has lectures [2]_____ the mornings. She has lunch [3]_____ 12.30. [4]_____ the afternoons, she works in the library. She watches television [5]_____ the evenings. She sees her friends [6]_____ weekends.

SPEAKING Study habits

1 Work with a partner. Match a verb in **A** with a word or phrase in **B**.

A		B
1 ☐ have		a) in the library
2 ☐ play		b) lunch
3 ☐ work		c) basketball
4 ☐ use		d) a computer

2 Label pictures 1–4 with a phrase from exercise 1.

3 🎵 3.6 Listen to the interview with Gina. What does she do? Find two activities in exercise 1.

4 Read the rules. Complete the interview with Gina.

A Excuse me, Gina!
B Yes?
A Could I ask you some questions about your study habits, please?
B OK.
A ¹_____ you a student here?
B Yes, I ²_____ .
A ³_____ you work in the library?
B Yes, I ⁴_____ .
A Do you use the computers here?
B No, I ⁵_____ .
A ⁶_____ you do any sport at the university?
B Yes, I ⁷_____ . I play basketball.
A Thank you.
B You're welcome.

RULES Present Simple (2) *yes / no* questions with short answers

With the verb *be*.

Are you a student?	Yes, **I am**.	No, **I'm not**.
Are you students?	Yes, **we are**.	No, **we're not**.
Are they students?	Yes, **they are**.	No, **they're not**.
Is he / **she** a student?	Yes, **he** / **she is**.	No, **he** / **she isn't**.

With other verbs, use *do* / *does* + verb.

Do you play football?	Yes, **I do**.	No, **I don't**.
Do they play football?	Yes, **they do**.	No, **they don't**.
Does he / **she** play football?	Yes, **he** / **she does**.	No, **he** / **she doesn't**.

---

5 🎵 3.6 Listen again and check your answers.

6 Work with a partner. Read the conversation aloud.

1

2

3

4

7 Work with a different partner. Ask and answer questions about Gina.

Is Gina a student?

Yes, she is.

Does she work in the library?

Yes, she does.

8 Read STUDY SKILL Circle four polite expressions in the interview in exercise 4 on page 18.

9 Add a polite expression to the conversations.

1 A Could I ask a question, _____?
   B Yes, of course.
   A When do we give in the homework?
   B On Monday morning.
   A _____.

2 A _____! Where's Room A5?
   B _____, I don't know.

3 A Thank you for your help.
   B _____.

🔊 3.7 Listen and check your answers.

10 Work with a partner. Practise the conversations.

11 Work with a partner. Ask and answer *yes/no* questions and questions with *When*. Use the ideas in the box.

Do you	use the computers at university? work in the library? do any sport? travel by bus?
When do you	go on Facebook? drive to university? go to the cafeteria? watch television?

12 Work with a different partner. Ask and answer questions about your partner in exercise 11.

Does Khalil travel by bus?

Yes, he does.

When does he work in the library?

At the weekend.

Does he go to the cafeteria?

I'm sorry, I don't know.

VOCABULARY DEVELOPMENT Words that go together

1 `Read STUDY SKILL` Look at Vocabulary record 1. Label the parts
with the words in the box.

> definition   example sentence   part of speech
> translation   word stress

STUDY SKILL Recording vocabulary (1)

It is important to record new vocabulary. Use a computer
file or a notebook to write down:

- the word stress.
- the part of speech.
- the translation.

- a definition.
- an example sentence.

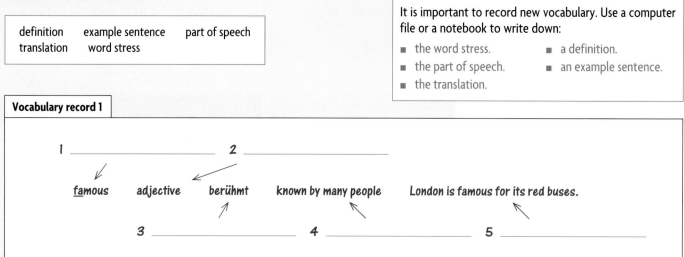

Vocabulary record 1

1 _____ 2 _____

famous   adjective   berühmt   known by many people   London is famous for its red buses.

3 _____   4 _____   5 _____

2 Complete Vocabulary record 2. Use a dictionary to help you.

Vocabulary record 2

Word	Part of speech	Translation	Definition	Example sentence
paragraph	*noun*			
improve				
semester				
large				
timetable				

3 `Read STUDY SKILL` Match the nouns with the verbs.

1 ☐ go   a) games
2 ☐ play   b) bus
3 ☐ use   c) television
4 ☐ watch   d) the Internet
5 ☐ travel by   e) shopping
6 ☐ go on   f) a computer

STUDY SKILL Recording vocabulary (2)

Some verbs and nouns are often used together:
use a computer, do homework

Record these words together to improve your
vocabulary.

4 Write three nouns in the box next to each verb. Use a dictionary to help you.

> computer games   an exam   an exercise
> football   a lecture   lunch   a seminar
> tennis   your work

play _____   _____   _____
do   _____   _____   _____
have _____   _____   _____

REVIEW

1 🔊 3.8 Listen and answer the question.

Do you hear about …?
a) Sonchai's studies
b) Sonchai's free time
c) Sonchai's studies and his free time

2 Complete the questions about Sonchai. Compare answers with a partner.

1 When / have lectures?

_____

2 When / use his computer?

_____

3 When / watch television?

_____

4 What sports / do?

_____

5 What / do after football?

_____

3 🔊 3.8 Listen again and answer the questions in exercise 2.

4 Complete the table for **You** with a time, part of the day, or day of the week.

When do you do these things?

	You	Partner 1	Partner 2
have breakfast			
have lunch			
study English			
drink coffee			
do sport			
go on the Internet			
talk to friends			
go shopping			

5 Work with two different partners. Take turns to ask and answer questions to complete the table. Remember to use polite expressions.

Excuse me! Could I ask you some questions?

4 Work

LISTENING SKILLS Understanding more than one speaker • Listening to discussions
SPEAKING SKILLS Giving opinions in discussions
VOCABULARY DEVELOPMENT Sounds and spelling (1) and (2)

LISTENING Under the sea and sand

1 Work in small groups. Answer the questions.

What are the good things and bad things about working
- outside?
- at night?
- away from home?

2 Work with a partner. Look at the pictures. What is the topic?

a) water
b) oil
c) gold

3 🎧 **4.1** Listen to the introduction to a podcast discussion. Check your answer to exercise 2.

4 **Read STUDY SKILL** 🎧 **4.2** Listen to part of the discussion. Answer the questions.

1 How many people are there?
2 How many men are there?
3 How many women are there?
4 Who are the speakers?

STUDY SKILL Understanding more than one speaker

It is difficult to understand when there is more than one speaker. Ask yourself questions about the speakers. This helps your understanding.

- Are they men or women?
- Do they sound different, e.g. do they have different accents?
- Who are the speakers, e.g. a teacher and a student, colleagues at work, an interviewer and a guest?

5 🔊 **4.2** Listen again. Write P for presenter, I for Dr Ikegama, and M for Dr Mehta. Who says …?

1 Good evening.
2 That's right.
3 Yes, I do.
4 Well, we work long hours.

6 🔊 **4.3** Listen to Dr Ikegama. Answer the questions. Check your answers with a partner.

1 What time does she start work?
2 What time does she finish work?
3 What is her main job?
4 What is important at sea?
5 Who does she have meetings with?

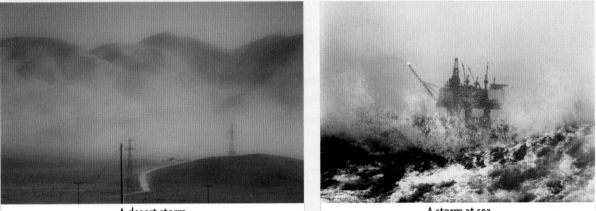

| A desert storm | A storm at sea |

7 `Read STUDY SKILL` 🔊 **4.4** Listen to the second part of the discussion. Are the sentences true (T) or false (F)?

1 ☐ Dr Mehta thinks long hours are bad.
2 ☐ Dr Ikegama doesn't think long hours are bad.
3 ☐ Dr Ikegama thinks working in bad weather is difficult.
4 ☐ Dr Mehta doesn't agree with Dr Ikegama.

STUDY SKILL Listening to discussions

In discussions in seminars and tutorials, people often give an opinion and a reason. They use expressions such as:
I think / I don't think / I believe … because …
I agree. / That's right.
Listening for these expressions helps you understand a discussion and people's opinions.

---

8 🔊 **4.4** Listen to the second part of the discussion again. Match an opinion with a reason. Write the sentences.

1 *Long hours are bad because …*

1 ☐ Long hours are bad		a) my colleagues are nice.
2 ☐ I enjoy working in the desert	because	b) I get very tired.
3 ☐ I miss my family		c) it's very beautiful.
4 ☐ I enjoy my work		d) I only see them four times a year.

SPEAKING Let's discuss it

1 Work with a partner. Look at the picture. Answer the questions.

  1 Where are the people?
  2 Who are they?
  3 Is it a) a presentation?
            b) a lecture?
            c) a discussion?

2 **Read STUDY SKILL** 4.5 Listen and tick (✓) the expressions for discussions you hear from the Language Bank.

LANGUAGE BANK Expressions for discussions	
Giving opinions	*I think … because …*
	I don't think … because …
Agreeing	*I agree.*
	That's right.
Disagreeing	*Sorry, I don't agree.*

STUDY SKILL Giving opinions in discussions

At college you discuss topics with your teacher and other students. In a discussion:
- give your opinion.
- listen to other people carefully.
- agree or disagree politely with other people's opinions.

3 4.5 Listen again. Number opinions a)–c) in the order you hear them, 1–3. Check your answers with a partner.

a) ☐ English is important because we use it for travelling.
b) ☐ English is important because most information on the Internet is in English.
c) ☐ English is important because it is the world language.

4 Work with a partner. Take turns to give opinions with reasons from the table.

I don't think being a doctor is a good job because you work long hours.

I think	being a doctor is a good job	because	you can use public transport.
			they are boring.
	cars are essential		you can help people.
			they are fun.
I don't think	computer games are great		they are quick.
			you work long hours.

5 (○) 4.6 Listen and number expressions a)–c) in the order you hear them, 1–3.

a) ☐ That's right.
b) ☐ I agree.
c) ☐ Sorry, I don't agree.

6 Work with a partner. Read the statements. Take turns to give your opinion and to agree or disagree. Use expressions from the Language Bank on page 24.

> I don't think it's important to go to university.

> Sorry, I don't agree.

1 It's not important to go to university.
2 It's a good idea to study science.
3 Friends are very important.
4 Fast food is good for you.
5 Shopping is fun.

7 Work with a partner. Take turns to give an opinion and to agree or disagree with ideas 1–3. Use the notes in brackets to help you.

A Give your opinion. Say why.
B Agree or disagree. Then give a new opinion. Say why.
A Agree or disagree.

Student A ideas
1 Television is good for children. (learn things / a lot of cartoons and films)
2 The Internet is a great invention. (a lot of information / uses a lot of time)
3 Watching films in English is good for learning. (fun / vocabulary not good)

> I think television is good for children because it helps them learn things.

> Sorry, I don't agree.

Student B ideas
1 Learning English is easy. (grammar simple / writing difficult)
2 Working with a partner is good. (discuss / same mistakes)
3 Doing a sport is good for you. (meet people / studying more important)

> I don't think learning English is easy because writing is difficult.

> I agree.

VOCABULARY DEVELOPMENT Spelling and pronunciation

1 🔊 4.7 Work with a partner. Listen to the sound of the *-s* at the end of the verbs. Are they the same (S) or different (D)? `Read STUDY SKILL`

   1 speak**s**   write**s** ___
   2 say**s**   use**s** ___
   3 watch**es**   cross**es** ___

2 Work with a partner. Say the verbs in the box aloud. Put them under the correct heading.

crosses	does	goes	helps	lives
teaches	thinks	watches	works	

/s/	/z/	/ɪz/
writes	leaves	washes

3 🔊 4.9 Listen and check your answers.

4 Work with a partner. Say three sentences aloud. Does your partner say the final *-s* correctly?

Student A
1 My father goes to work by car.
2 My sister works for an oil company.
3 My aunt teaches at the university.

Student B
1 My mother does art classes.
2 My cousin lives in New York.
3 My brother watches a lot of television.

5 🔊 4.10 Listen and check your answers.

6 `Read STUDY SKILL` Underline the consonants at the beginning of the words in Groups A–D.

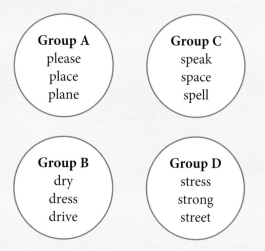

Group A
please
place
plane

Group C
speak
space
spell

Group B
dry
dress
drive

Group D
stress
strong
street

7 Work with a partner. Say the words in exercise 6 aloud.

8 🔊 4.12 Listen and check.

STUDY SKILL Sounds and spelling (1)

Look at the final *-s* in the 3rd person singular of the Present Simple. We pronounce it in three ways:

■ for some verbs it is a /s/ sound.
   write /raɪt/ write**s** /raɪts/

■ for some verbs it is a /z/ sound.
   leave /liːv/ leave**s** /liːvz/

■ for verbs ending in *-ch, -ss, -sh, -z, -s, -x* it is an /ɪz/ sound.
   wash /wɒʃ/ wash**es** /wɒʃɪz/

🔊 4.8 Listen.

Write the correct pronunciation when you record a new verb.

STUDY SKILL Sounds and spelling (2)

Many English words start with two or three consonants, e.g. *play*, *black*, *three*, *screen*.

■ Say the consonants together. Do not add an extra vowel sound.
   play /pleɪ/ NOT /pəleɪ/
   screen /skriːn/ NOT /səkriːn/

  🔊 4.11 Listen.

■ Use a dictionary to find the correct pronunciation.

REVIEW

1 Work with a partner. Look at the pictures. What is the topic?

  a) working at night
  b) working at home
  c) working and travelling

2 🎧 **4.13** Listen to the introduction to a discussion. Check your answer to exercise 1.

3 🎧 **4.14** Listen to part of the discussion. Answer the questions.

  1 How many people are there?
  2 How many women are there?

4 🎧 **4.14** Listen again and answer the questions. Compare your answers with your partner.

  1 Who thinks working at home is good?
    a) the man   b) the woman

  2 Who doesn't think working at home is good?
    a) the man   b) the woman

  3 Why does Steven have this opinion?
    a) Because he can choose his working time.
    b) Because he works long hours.

  4 Why does Laura have this opinion?
    a) Because she doesn't meet people.
    b) Because she works long hours.

5 Work with a partner. Decide if you agree (A) or disagree (D) with the sentences.

A good salary is very important. ___	**Sports stars get too much money.** ___

6 Choose one sentence from exercise 5. Think of three reasons to support your opinion.

7 Work in small groups. Take turns to give your opinions and reasons. Agree or disagree politely with the people in your group.

5 Different kinds of language

LISTENING SKILLS Understanding a lecture • Using visuals (1)
SPEAKING SKILLS Giving a presentation (1)
VOCABULARY DEVELOPMENT Sounds and spelling (3)
RESEARCH Researching a topic (1) and (2)

LISTENING The language of dots

1 Work in small groups. Answer the questions.

1 Which languages do you speak?
2 Which languages do children learn at school in your country?
3 Which languages do you think are important today? Why?

2 `Read STUDY SKILLS REVIEW` Look at the notice for a lecture. What is the lecture about? Make questions.

1 what / braille?   **What is braille?**
2 who / it for?
3 how / people use it?
4 / different ways / writing braille?

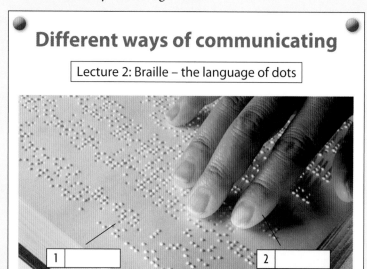

Different ways of communicating

Lecture 2: Braille – the language of dots

1   2

Tuesday, 10.00 a.m.
Room 9

STUDY SKILLS REVIEW Understanding a lecture

To understand a lecture or a talk well:
- decide what information you need before you listen. (see Study Skill p4)
- predict information from the title and any pictures. (see Study Skill p10)
- listen for the general idea. (see Study Skill p16)
- listen for detail, e.g. important words and numbers. (see Study Skill p5)

3 Label the picture in the notice with the words in the box.

> dots   finger

4 5.1 Listen to the first part of the lecture and tick (✓) the topics you hear.

1 ☐ Reading and writing braille
2 ☐ Braille in different languages
3 ☐ The history of braille

5 5.1 Listen again and answer the questions in exercise 2.

6 5.2 Listen to the second part of the lecture. What two topics about braille does the speaker discuss?

7 **Read STUDY SKILL** Read the questions. Look at Slides 1 and 2. Which questions can you answer from the information in the slides?

1 How many dots are there in the letter 'a'?
2 Where are the dots in the letter 'c'?
3 How many dots are there in the letter 'x'?
4 How many positions are there for the dots?
5 What is the sign for a capital letter in braille?
6 Does the sign for a capital letter go before or after the letter?

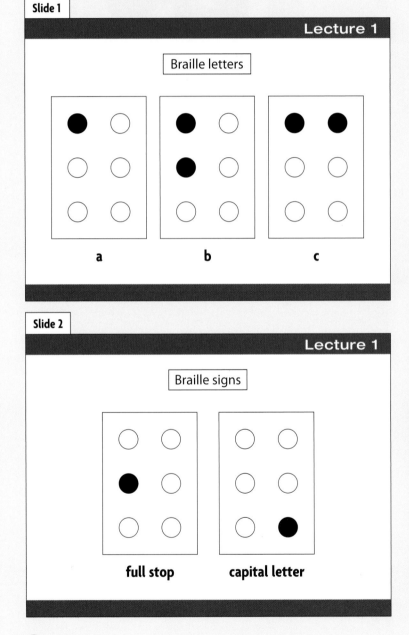

Slide 1 — Lecture 1 — Braille letters: a, b, c

Slide 2 — Lecture 1 — Braille signs: full stop, capital letter

8 5.2 Listen again and answer the questions in exercise 7.

SPEAKING Body language

1 Work in small groups. Are these good things to do in a presentation? Why (not)?

- Speak clearly.
- Sit down.
- Hold your notes in front of your face.
- Look at your listeners.
- Smile.

I think it is important to speak clearly because it helps your listeners.

2 **Read STUDY SKILLS REVIEW** Which advice for giving a presentation is most important for you? Compare with a partner.

> ### STUDY SKILLS REVIEW Giving a presentation (1)
>
> **When you give a presentation:**
> - start and finish your talk well. (see Study Skill p13)
> - speak clearly and slowly. (see Study Skill p13)
> - smile and be polite. (see Study Skill p19)
> - listen carefully and agree or disagree politely. (see Study Skill p24)

3 🎧 **5.3** Listen to two students give an introduction to a talk. Is speaker 1 or speaker 2 better? Why? Discuss your answers with a partner.

4 Read and complete the introduction to the talk.

> 66 Good ¹_____. My ²_____ is Akemi. My ³_____ today is ⁴_____ body language. This is when people use their eyes and their hands to give more information. We all use body language when we speak, for ⁵_____, in presentations or discussions. Body language is different in different cultures, for example … 99

5 (5.4) Listen and compare your answers. Practise reading the introduction to yourself. Think of one example from your own country.

6 Work with a partner. Practise giving the talk. Think about:
- pauses at the ends of sentences.
- good body language.

7 Work in small groups. Take turns to give the talk. Answer the questions about your partners.
- Did they speak clearly?
- Did they pause at the ends of sentences?
- Did they use good body language?
- Was the example interesting?

8 Work with a partner. Student A, look at page 74.
Student B, look at page 77.

VOCABULARY DEVELOPMENT Silent letters

1 ❚ Read STUDY SKILL ❚ (5.6) Listen to the words. Cross out the silent letter(s).

answer   answ~~e~~r

lamb

light

business

half

hour

friend

> **STUDY SKILL** Sounds and spelling (3)
>
> Some words have silent letters. These are letters which are not pronounced.
>
> *listen* /lɪsən/
> *watch* /wɒtʃ/
>
> (5.5) Listen.
>
> Cross out the silent letter or write the phonetics when you record these words.
>
> lis~~t~~en /lɪsən/

2 Work with a partner. Take turns to say the words in exercise 1 aloud.

3 Record the words in exercise 1 in your notebook with the phonetics, or the silent letter crossed out.

autumn

eight

island

know

write

RESEARCH Websites

1 Read STUDY SKILL Read the homework task. Use the question words to write four questions about the inventor of braille.

| Who?   Where?   Why?   When? |

| Ways of communicating |
| Week 4 Homework task 2 – Prepare a two-minute talk about the inventor of braille. |

STUDY SKILL Researching a topic (1)

Researching a topic on the Internet can be difficult because there is a lot of information to read. Decide what information you need. Write questions to find this information.

Topic: Sign language
Questions: *What is sign language? Who uses it?*

2 Compare your questions with a partner.

3 Use the Internet to research the answers to your questions in exercise 1.

4 Compare your answers with a partner.

5 Read the homework task. Use the question words to write three questions to find information about the Spanish language.

| How many people?   Which countries?   How many letters? |

| Ways of communicating |
| Week 4 Homework task 3 – A presentation. Do research for a two-minute talk on the Spanish language. |

6 Read STUDY SKILL Use the Internet to research the answers to your questions in exercise 5. Make a note of the website(s) you used.

STUDY SKILL Researching a topic (2)

Remember to make a note of the website you use and the date that you use it.

http://brailleinformation.org *(20 September 2012)*

http://non-verbalcommunication.org *(20 September 2012)*

7 Compare your answers with a partner.

REVIEW

1 Work with a partner. Look at the notice for the lecture and the slides. What is the lecture about?

2 Make questions using the words.
   1 what / for?
   2 who uses / ?
   3 what two signals / stop?
   4 what signal / go?

3 Label the pictures in the slides with the words in the box.

back of the hand   left arm   palm of the hand   right arm

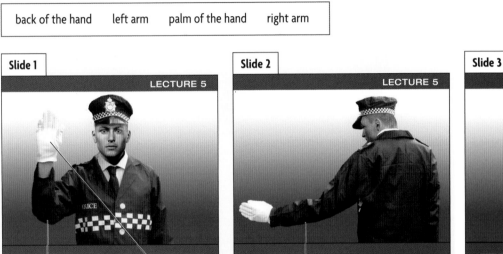

Different ways of communicating

Lecture 5: Hand signals

4 🔊 5.7 Listen and tick (✓) the topics you hear.
   ☐ The hand signal for stop
   ☐ The hand signal for go
   ☐ The hand signal for turn right

5 🔊 5.7 Listen again to the lecture. Answer the questions in exercise 2. Compare your answers with your partner.

6 Read the homework task. Choose a language and write questions to find information about it.

> <u>Homework task</u>
> Give a short talk about Hindi, Portuguese, or Russian.

7 Use the Internet to research the answers to your questions in exercise 6. Make a note of the websites you use and the date you use them.

8 Write a short talk about the language. Remember to introduce your talk correctly. Practise giving your talk.

9 Work with two students. Take turns to give your talk. Think about:
   • pauses at the ends of sentences.
   • good body language.

6 The importance of studying

LISTENING SKILLS Understanding the structure of a talk • Recognizing pauses
SPEAKING SKILLS Helping the listener (2) and (3)
VOCABULARY DEVELOPMENT Word-building (1) • Using a dictionary (2)

LISTENING Pi

1 Work in small groups. Answer the questions.

1 What was your best subject at school?
2 What was your worst subject at school?
3 At what age can children choose the subjects they study at school?

2 Work with a partner. Read the title of the seminar. Look at Figures 1 and 2. What do you know about pi?

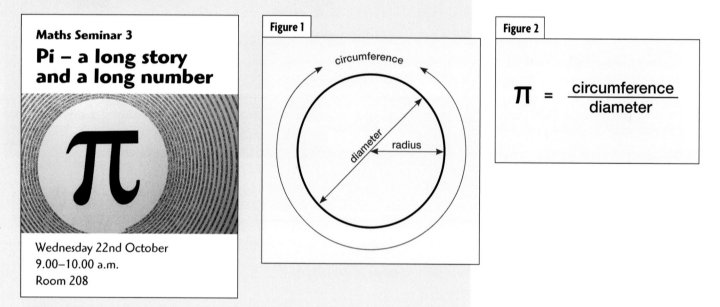

Maths Seminar 3
Pi – a long story and a long number

Wednesday 22nd October
9.00–10.00 a.m.
Room 208

Figure 1

circumference

diameter

radius

Figure 2

$$\pi = \frac{circumference}{diameter}$$

3 6.1 Listen to the introduction to the seminar on pi. Number the topics in the order you hear them, 1–4.

☐ The uses of pi
☐ The history of pi
☐ What pi is
☐ Why it is called pi

4 **Read STUDY SKILL** Write the word that shows the correct order next to the topics in exercise 3.

finally	firstly	secondly	then

5 6.1 Listen again and check your answers.

> **STUDY SKILL** Understanding the structure of a talk
>
> Good speakers structure their talks clearly. They use words to introduce new ideas:
> *firstly, ...   secondly, ...   then ...   finally, ...*
>
> Listening for these words helps you understand the order of information in a talk.

6 🎧 6.2 Listen to the seminar. Choose the correct answer.

1 What is the approximate value of pi?
   a) 3.14   b) 3.41
2 Why is it called pi?
   a) pi means 'circumference' in Greek
   b) pi is the first letter of the Greek word for 'circumference'
3 Who first used pi?
   a) the Greeks   b) the Egyptians
4 How many digits did Liu Hui calculate pi to?
   a) 4 digits   b) 3 digits
5 How many digits can we calculate pi to today?
   a) millions   b) trillions
6 What do we use pi for?
   a) calculations in maths only
   b) calculations in maths, science, and engineering

7 **Read STUDY SKILL** 🎧 6.3 Look at the first part of the seminar. Listen and write a slash (/) where the speaker pauses.

> ❝ Firstly, / what is pi? / Well, pi is a useful number because it helps us make calculations about circles. Pi is the circumference of a circle divided by the diameter. It is approximately 3.14. This number is true for all circles.
>
> And why is it called pi? A British mathematician, William Jones, called it pi because pi is the first letter of the Greek word which means 'circumference'. ❞

STUDY SKILL Recognizing pauses

Good speakers pause after a group of words to make their talk clear. Recognizing these pauses helps you understand.

8 🎧 6.4 Listen to the introduction to a lecture on mathematicians. Number the pictures in the order you hear the names.

Albert Einstein

Pythagoras

Isaac Newton

9 🎧 6.4 Listen again and write a slash (/) where the speaker pauses.

> ❝ Good morning. / My lecture today is about famous mathematicians. Firstly, I'm going to discuss the work of Isaac Newton. Secondly, I'm going to talk about Albert Einstein. And finally, we're going to look at Pythagoras and how his work influences modern maths today. ❞

SPEAKING What we study

1 Work in small groups. Discuss the questions.

1 When do you use maths in your life?
2 Which jobs use maths?
3 Why is maths important?

2 Complete the introduction to a talk on maths in different jobs. Use the words that show order. **Read STUDY SKILL**

finally	firstly	secondly	then

STUDY SKILL Helping the listener (2)

Help your listeners understand your talk.

- Say what the talk is about: *My talk today is about …*
- Organize the talk using words that show order: *firstly, secondly, then, finally*
- Say what topics you are going to talk about: *Firstly, I'm going to discuss / talk about / look at maths in engineering.*

Maths

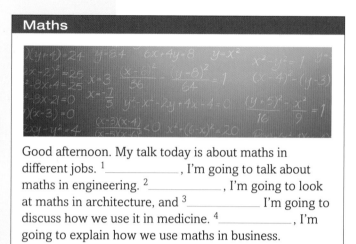

Good afternoon. My talk today is about maths in different jobs. ¹_____, I'm going to talk about maths in engineering. ²_____, I'm going to look at maths in architecture, and ³_____ I'm going to discuss how we use it in medicine. ⁴_____, I'm going to explain how we use maths in business.

3 🔊 6.5 Listen and check your answers to exercise 2.

4 Work with a partner. Student A, give an introduction to a talk on sport. Student B, give an introduction to a talk on business. Use the topics.

Good morning/afternoon. Today I'm going to give a talk about sport/business.

Student A

Sport

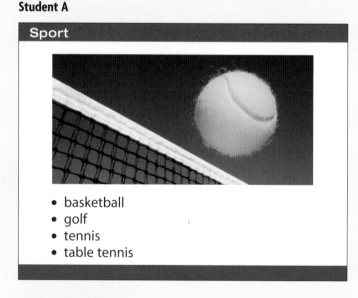

- basketball
- golf
- tennis
- table tennis

Student B

Business

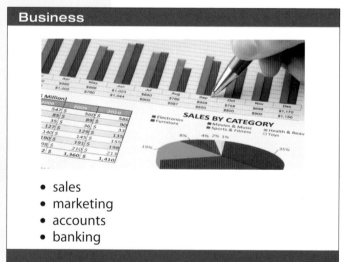

- sales
- marketing
- accounts
- banking

5 **Read STUDY SKILL** 🔊 6.5 Listen again to the introduction in exercise 2. Write a slash (/) where the speaker pauses.

STUDY SKILL Helping the listener (3)

When you say long sentences, it is important to pause after each idea. This makes your sentences easier to understand.
The Egyptians first used pi / about 4,000 years ago / to build their pyramids.

🔊 6.6 Listen.

6 Work with a partner. Look again at exercise 2 on page 36.
Take turns to read the introduction aloud with the correct pauses.

7 Choose an academic subject. Think of four topic areas in that subject.

Academic subject:
1
2
3
4

8 Prepare the introduction to a talk on your subject. Remember to:
- introduce your subject.
- use words that show the order of the topics.
- pause after each idea.

9 Work in small groups. Take turns to give the introduction to your talk.

VOCABULARY DEVELOPMENT Word families

1 Work with a partner. Read sentences 1–3. Look at the underlined words.
Which one is:
- ☐ a noun (person)?
- ☐ a noun (thing)?
- ☐ a verb?

1 Mathematics is the <u>study</u> of numbers.
2 Einstein <u>studied</u> physics in Switzerland.
3 Einstein taught many <u>students</u> during his life.

2 **Read STUDY SKILL** Add the words in the box to the table.

| lecturer | use | worker | writing |

verb	noun (thing)	noun (person)
<u>study</u>	a <u>study</u>	a <u>student</u>
_____	an in<u>ven</u>tion	an _____
work	_____	a _____
_____	a use	a _____
_____	_____	a <u>writer</u>
_____	a <u>lecture</u>	a _____

STUDY SKILL Word-building (1)

Some words are part of a word family. There is a verb form of the word and one or more noun forms (a person, place, or thing).

teach   verb
a teacher   noun (person)
teaching   noun (thing)

Make a note of words from the same word family. This helps increase your vocabulary.

3 `Read STUDY SKILL` Work with a partner. Complete the table in exercise 2 on page 37. Underline the stressed syllable. Use a dictionary to help you.

4 6.7 Listen and check your answers to exercise 3.

5 Work with a partner. Practise saying the words in the table in exercise 2.

6 6.8 Complete the sentences with a word from the table on page 37. Listen and check your answers.

1 My brother teaches at a university. He's a _____ in economics.
2 I use a computer to _____ my essays.
3 Many people worked on the _____ of the Internet.
4 I would like to _____ law at university.

7 Work with a partner. Use a dictionary to complete the word families.

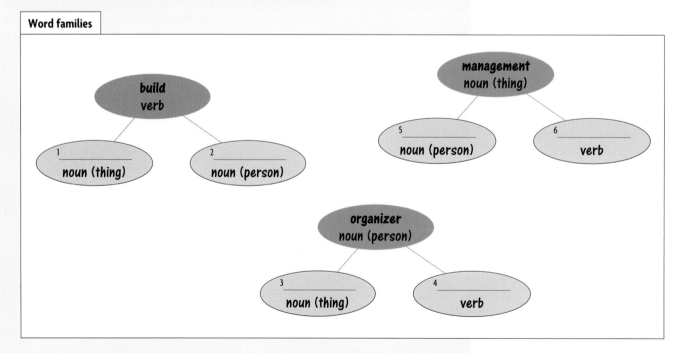

Word families

build
verb

1 _____ noun (thing)

2 _____ noun (person)

management
noun (thing)

5 _____ noun (person)

6 _____ verb

organizer
noun (person)

3 _____ noun (thing)

4 _____ verb

REVIEW

1 Work in small groups. Read the title of the lecture. Discuss the questions.

   1 What is the lecture about?

   2 What is higher education?

   3 Why do people study in higher education?

LECTURE	ROOM	DATE	TIME
The importance of studying in higher education	Lecture theatre 54	23rd November	3.00

2 6.9 Listen to the introduction to the lecture. Number the topics 1–3 in the order you hear them. Check your answers with a partner.

   ☐ Reasons for studying in higher education

   ☐ What higher education is

   ☐ Courses and qualifications in higher education

3 6.9 Listen to the introduction to the lecture again. Write a slash (/) where the speaker pauses.

> ❝ Good afternoon. / My talk today / is about the importance of studying in higher education. Firstly, I'm going to look at what higher education is. Secondly, I'm going to talk about courses and qualifications. And finally, I'm going to give you the reasons for studying in higher education. ❞

4 Work with a partner. Take turns to read the introduction to the lecture in exercise 3 aloud.

5 6.10 Listen to the lecture. Are the sentences true (**T**) or false (**F**)?

   1 ☐ All higher education institutions are universities.

   2 ☐ A course is usually in three subjects.

   3 ☐ You can get a degree or a diploma in higher education.

   4 ☐ Some people choose a subject because they need it for a job.

   5 ☐ You can often get a good job with a higher education qualification.

6 Choose an academic subject. Think of four jobs you can do after studying this subject.

Academic subject:	
Jobs 1	
2	
3	
4	

7 Prepare an introduction to a talk on your subject and the jobs you can do.

8 Work in small groups. Take turns to give the introduction to your talk. Listen to your partners' talks. Write the jobs they talk about.

7 Developments in technology

LISTENING SKILLS Taking notes (1) • Listening for explanations
KEY LANGUAGE Saying dates (1) and (2)
SPEAKING SKILLS Helping the listener (4)
VOCABULARY DEVELOPMENT Sounds and spelling (4) • Word-building (2)

LISTENING Technology and telephones

1 Make a list of the electronic equipment you have.

MP3 player …

2 Compare your list with your partner. Do you have the same things?

3 Work with a partner. Look at the advertisement for a podcast. Answer the questions.

1 What is the name of the series?
2 What is the name of the programme?
3 How long is the podcast?

> **Series: Technology then and now**
>
> **1 Telephone technology – the history of the smartphone**
>
> 🎧 Last updated: 15 hours ago
>
> 🕐 Duration: 35 minutes

4 | Read STUDY SKILL | 🔊 7.1 Listen to the start of the podcast. Complete headings A, B, and C in the notes.

THE HISTORY OF THE SMARTPHONE		
A Who? Four famous _____	B _____ they developed	C _____ (dates)
IBM	Simon phone – calendar, address book, notepad, email	1 _____
Nokia	Nokia 9000 – 2 _____ and PDA	1996
Ericsson	E380 – used the word 3 _____ for 1st time	4 _____
5 _____	iPhone – today more than 500,000 apps	2007

> **STUDY SKILL** Taking notes (1)
>
> Taking notes helps you remember important information. Always listen to the start of the talk. This helps you decide how to organize the notes. Use:
> - headings.
> - years / dates.

5 🔊 7.2 Listen to the podcast. Complete the notes in exercise 4.

6 **Read STUDY SKILL** 🎧 7.3 Read and listen to sentences from the podcast. Complete the sentences with expressions in the box.

in other words or that is

1 This was a phone and a PDA, _____, a Personal Digital Assistant.
2 Applications, _____ apps, used 4MB.
3 There were 2MB for personal data, _____, personal information.

> **STUDY SKILL** Listening for explanations
>
> Good speakers explain new or difficult words. Listen for expressions such as *or*, *that is*, *in other words*.
> *The IBM Simon phone weighed 1lb 2oz,* **that is**, *about half a kilogram.*
>
> This helps you understand new vocabulary.

7 🎧 7.4 Listen to part of a podcast about television. Tick (✓) the words and expressions the speaker explains. Compare your answers with a partner.

☐ television
☐ monochrome
☐ worldwide
☐ flat screen
☐ took off

8 🎧 7.4 Listen again and write the meanings of the words and phrases.

1 monochrome	
2 worldwide	
3 took off	

Marconi TV, 1938

Braun TV, 1955

Flatscreen TV, c. 2000

KEY LANGUAGE Dates

1 🎧 7.5 Listen and tick (✓) the year you hear. `Read STUDY SKILL`

1 ☐ a) 1948
   ☐ b) 1938
2 ☐ a) 1705
   ☐ b) 1605
3 ☐ a) 2012
   ☐ b) 2020
4 ☐ a) 2000
   ☐ b) 200

STUDY SKILL Saying dates (1)

It is important to say dates clearly.

■ For years, say pairs of numbers.
   Write *1994*, say *19* (nineteen) *94* (ninety-four).

■ For years with a zero, say *oh*.
   Write *1905*, say *19* (nineteen) *05* (oh five).

---

2 Work with a partner. Take turns to say a year from exercise 1. Underline the years your partner says.

3 🎧 7.6 Listen and write the years you hear. Compare your answers with your partner.

1 _____
2 _____
3 _____
4 _____
5 _____

4 🎧 7.7 Read and listen to the dates. What is different about the way we write and say dates? `Read STUDY SKILL`

1st January
19th March
22nd August

STUDY SKILL Saying dates (2)

■ For dates in a month, use ordinal numbers.
   Write *21st January*, say **the** *twenty-first* **of** *January*.

■ For centuries, also use ordinal numbers.
   Write *the 16th century*, say *the sixteenth century*.

---

5 Work with a partner. Student A, look at page 74. Student B, look at page 77.

1268

1402

1547

1999

2015

2025

31st January

14th March

17th Century

SPEAKING Telecommunications

1 Work in small groups. Write a list of ways you can communicate with people.

talking

2 Work with a partner. Add the information in the box to the timeline.

> Berners-Lee   the telephone   1973   1892

Topic: Important developments in the history of telecommunications

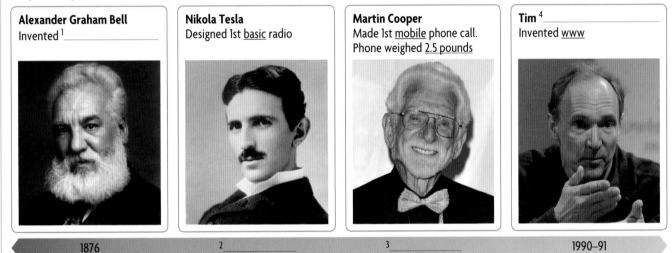

Alexander Graham Bell
Invented ¹_____

Nikola Tesla
Designed 1st <u>basic</u> radio

Martin Cooper
Made 1st <u>mobile</u> phone call.
Phone weighed <u>2.5 pounds</u>

Tim ⁴_____
Invented <u>www</u>

1876   2_____   3_____   1990–91

---

3 **Read STUDY SKILL** 🔊 7.8 Listen to the start of a talk on the history of telecommunications. Answer the questions.
1 Does the speaker say the topic of the talk?
2 Does the speaker explain any words? What word(s)?

4 Match a word from the timeline in exercise 2 with its explanation.

1 ☐ basic   a) World Wide Web
2 ☐ www   b) 1.1 kilos
3 ☐ 2.5 pounds   c) can be carried
4 ☐ mobile   d) simple

5 Work with a partner. Take turns to explain words 1–4 from exercise 4. Use an expression from the Study Skill.

6 Prepare and practise a short talk to describe the events on the timeline in exercise 2. Remember:
1 Say the topic. *My talk is about …*
2 Order the information in the talk, using *firstly*, *secondly*, *then*, and *finally*.
3 Rephrase the underlined words and expressions in the timeline, using *or*, *that is*, and *in other words*.

7 Work with a different partner. Take turns to give the talk. Did your partner:
1 tell you the topic?
2 organize the talk?
3 say years and dates clearly?
4 explain words?

8 Work with a partner. Student A, look at page 74. Student B, look at page 77.

STUDY SKILL Helping the listener (4)

Help your listeners to understand your talk by explaining new or difficult words. Use expressions such as *or*, *that is*, *in other words*.

VOCABULARY DEVELOPMENT Past Simple endings

1 🔊 7.9 Listen to the verbs. What are the different sounds for the -ed ending? `Read STUDY SKILL`

discover**ed**   start**ed**   cross**ed**

2 Work with a partner. Say the verbs and put them under the correct heading.

| added | appeared | called | helped | invented |
| liked | looked | organized | tried | |

/d/	/ɪd/	/t/

3 🔊 7.11 Listen and check your answers.

Compound nouns

4 `Read STUDY SKILL` Match a noun 1–5 with a)–e) to make compound nouns.

1 ☐ web   a) chip
2 ☐ word   b) stick
3 ☐ address   c) page
4 ☐ memory   d) processor
5 ☐ computer   e) book

5 🔊 7.12 Listen and check your answers. Practise saying the words.

6 Work with a partner. Underline the stressed syllable in the compound nouns. Practise saying the words.

1 keyboard
2 headphones
3 home page
4 laptop
5 touchscreen
6 computer game

7 🔊 7.13 Listen and check your answers.

STUDY SKILL Sounds and spelling (4)

Regular verbs in the Past Simple end with -ed. We say this in three ways.

- /d/ for most verbs: *live – lived* /lɪvd/
- /ɪd/ for verbs ending with a /t/ or /d/ sound: *want – wanted* /ˈwɒntɪd/ *decide – decided* /dɪˈsaɪdɪd/
- /t/ for verbs ending in -sh, -ch, -s, -k, -p sounds: *watch – watched* /wɒtʃt/

🔊 7.10 Listen.

Write the Past Simple sound when you record new verbs.

STUDY SKILL Word-building (2)

Some nouns are made of two nouns together, e.g. *motorbike = motor + bike*. These are called compound nouns. They can be written as one word or two words: *whiteboard, mouse mat*.

- The stress is usually on the first noun: *whiteboard   mouse mat*
- Use a dictionary to find the correct stress (').

REVIEW

1 Work in small groups. Look at the pictures. Answer the questions.
  1 Who are the people? Where are they?
  2 Do you have a video game console?
    If yes, which games do you have? / If no, why not?

PlayStation   Wii   Xbox

2 🎧 7.14 Listen to the introduction to a podcast about video game consoles.
Tick (✓) the names of the companies you hear.

☐ Atari   ☐ Microsoft   ☐ Mattel
☐ Nintendo   ☐ Sega   ☐ Sony

3 🎧 7.15 Listen to the podcast and complete the notes on the timeline.

Microsoft	Sony	4 _____
Xbox 360	PlayStation 3	Wii
USA	2 _____	North 5 _____

◄──►
ˡ_____ 2005   11th November ³_____   19th November 2006

4 Compare your answers with a partner.

5 🎧 7.16 Listen to part of the podcast again. Write the explanation of
the words.

| seventh generation | |
| compatible | |

6 You are going to prepare a 1–2 minute talk on technology. Your teacher will
give you a topic.
  1 Research your topic on the Internet (see Study Skills p32). Find three
    important developments.
  2 Prepare your talk. Think about:
    • starting and ending well.
    • organizing the information.
    • speaking slowly and clearly.
    • your body language.

7 Work in small groups. Take turns to give your talks. Make notes on your
partners' talks using headings or timelines.

LISTENING SKILLS   Taking notes (2)   •   Listening for questions
SPEAKING SKILLS   Helping the listener (5)   •   Asking for help (3)
RESEARCH   Finding information (1) and (2)

LISTENING   Big business

1   Work in small groups. Answer the questions.

1   What cars are popular in your country?
2   Do they make cars in your country?
3   How many people do you think work in the car industry worldwide?
   • 100 million
   • 150 million
   • 200 million
4   What different kinds of vehicles are there?

2   Work with a partner. Look at the notice. What is the seminar about? Tick (✓) the ideas you think the speaker is going to talk about.

☐ number of vehicles
☐ luxury cars
☐ number of people in the industry
☐ amount of money in the industry

Seminar 1
The car industry – a big business

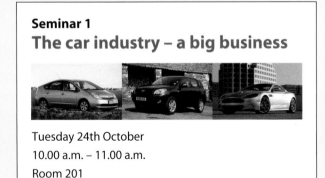

Tuesday 24th October
10.00 a.m. – 11.00 a.m.
Room 201

3   🎧 8.1 Listen to the introduction to the seminar presentation. Were your answers in exercise 2 correct?

4 **Read STUDY SKILL** 🎵 8.2 Listen to the first part of the presentation. Listen for the main idea, reasons, and examples. Complete the notes.

THE CAR INDUSTRY

Main idea 1: The car industry is very large.

Reasons: Many people want to have a car.

Many people ^1_____ buy a car.

Examples: Number of vehicles: ^2_____ million a year

Number of people: ^3_____ million

Amount of money: $ ^4_____ billion a year

STUDY SKILL Taking notes (2)

A speaker often gives a main idea, or general topic, and then supports the idea with reasons and examples.

Main idea: *The … industry is a very large international business.*

Reason: *… because … is / are popular around the world.*

Examples: *There are … factories.*
It makes … euros / dollars a year.
It employs … people.

Make notes of the main ideas, supporting reasons, and examples.

5 Compare your answers with a partner.

6 **Read STUDY SKILL** 🎵 8.3 Match the two parts of the questions. Then listen to the second part of the presentation and check your answers.

1 ☐ Excuse me, could you repeat
2 ☐ Excuse me, could I
3 ☐ Sorry, could you give

a) me an example of that?
b) that number, please?
c) ask you a question?

STUDY SKILL Listening for questions

If you have problems understanding a talk or presentation, listen for other people's questions and the speaker's answers. These can help you understand.

7 🎵 8.3 Listen again and complete the notes.

Main idea 2: The car industry is very international.

Reason: Car companies make and sell cars in ^1_____ worldwide.

Examples: ^2_____ countries produce cars.

Chile makes ^3_____ vehicles a year.

China produces ^4_____ of vehicles a year.

Main idea 3: Toyota is very ^5_____.

Reasons: ^6_____, _____ cars Example: Yaris

^7_____ quality cars Example: very few mechanical problems

^8_____ about the future Examples: hybrid and ^9_____ cars

Car production line, China

8 Compare your answers with a partner.

SPEAKING The clothing industry

1 Work with a partner. Look at the pictures. Answer the questions.

   1 What do these companies sell?
   2 Do these companies have shops in your town?
   3 Who buys their products?

2 `Read STUDY SKILL` Complete the talk with the words in the box.

> | because   for example (x 2)   such as |
> |---|

> 66 There are many parts to the clothing industry. I am going to talk about one part: designer labels, ¹_____, Gucci, Prada, and Ralph Lauren. These companies make a lot of products, ²_____ clothes, handbags, and jewellery. Designer labels are very popular ³_____ they use good quality materials and the products are fashionable. But they can be quite expensive. ⁴_____, a pair of Armani jeans can cost nearly 500 euros. 99

STUDY SKILL Helping the listener (5)

Make sure your talk has a clear main idea. Support this main idea with reasons and examples.

- For reasons, use *because*:
  *It is very international **because** today car companies make and sell cars in many countries worldwide.*

- For examples, use *such as, for example*:
  *Some of these countries, **such as** Chile, make about five thousand vehicles a year.*
  ***For example**, China produces millions of vehicles.*

3 🔘 8.4 Listen and check your answers.

4 `Read STUDY SKILL` Match a sentence 1–3 with a question asking for help a)–c).

   1 ☐ These companies make a lot of products.
   2 ☐ Designer labels are very popular because they use good quality materials.
   3 ☐ A pair of Armani jeans can cost nearly 500 euros.

   a) Sorry, could you give me an example of the materials?
   b) Could you repeat the price, please?
   c) Excuse me, could I ask a question? What do they make?

STUDY SKILL Asking for help (3)

If you want more information, interrupt politely. Say:
Sorry, could you give me an example (of that)?
Excuse me, could you repeat that / the (…), please?
Excuse me, could I ask (you) a question?

5 🔘 8.5 Listen and check your answers.

Designer labels

6 Work with a partner. Take turns to say sentences 1–3. Ask for more information with a question from exercise 4 on page 48.

1 230,000 people work for the company.
2 The company produces many different electronic products.
3 That is the end of my talk.

7 Work with a partner. Organize the notes about the company Giorgio Armani under the headings.

GIORGIO ARMANI
It sells to different customers.
It develops new business projects.
It sells to famous people, business people, and young people.
Giorgio Armani is a successful company.
It makes different products.
It makes clothes, shoes, watches, and furniture.
It opens new luxury hotels in big cities.

Main idea:	
Reason 1	Example:
Reason 2	Example:
Reason 3	Example:

The Armani Hotel, Dubai

8 Practise saying the information in the correct order. Start with the main idea.

9 Work with a partner. Take turns to be Student A and Student B. Follow the instructions. Use the notes in exercise 7.

Student A	Student B
1 Say the main idea. Give a reason.	2 Interrupt and ask for an example.
3 Give an example.	4 Ask Student A to repeat it.
5 Repeat the example and give another reason.	6 Interrupt and say you want to ask a question. Ask a question.
7 Answer the question. Finish your talk.	

10 Work with a partner. Student A, look at page 75. Student B, look at page 78.

RESEARCH Independent learning

1 [Read STUDY SKILL] Work with a partner. Look at the online dictionary entries for *seminar* and *employ*. Answer the questions.

1 What part of speech are they?
2 Underline the definitions.
3 Find the example sentences.
4 Say the words with the correct stress.

> **seminar** /ˈsemɪnɑː(r)/ *noun* a small class at university where students discuss a subject with a teacher: *I have a seminar on the car industry this afternoon.*

> **employ** /ɪmˈplɔɪ/ *verb* to pay somebody to do work: *The company employs 100 people.*

2 Use an online dictionary to look up the words in the box. Write the part of speech and a definition.

> company   factory   industry

3 Compare your answers with your partner.

4 [Read STUDY SKILL] Use a website or app to find the words in the box. Listen and mark the word stress.

> develop   engine   produce   vehicle

> ### STUDY SKILL Finding information (2)
>
> You can use some websites and apps (applications) to hear how a word sounds in English. Click on the icon  to hear the word. Mark the word stress in your notebook or computer file.

5 Write the definition and an example sentence for each word in exercise 4.

6 Work with a partner. Compare your answers. Take turns to say the words aloud.

> ### STUDY SKILL Finding information (1)
>
> When you are working on a computer, it is often quick and easy to use an online dictionary to find information about a word in English. A dictionary entry will give you:
>
> - the part of speech.
> - a definition.
> - the word stress.
> - the pronunciation.
> - an example sentence.

REVIEW

1 Work in small groups. Answer the questions.

   1 Name the 'fast food' in the pictures.
   2 What kind of fast food is popular in your country?
   3 Do you like eating fast food? Why (not)?

2 Work with a partner. Look at the notice. What is the seminar about? What type of food does Subway make?

3 8.6 Listen to the introduction to the presentation. What is the main idea of the presentation?

   ☐ a history of Subway   ☐ the success of Subway
   ☐ the Subway restaurants

> **Seminar 2**
> ## A fast food company – Subway
> Tuesday 21st November
> 2.00 p.m.
> The Green Room

4 8.7 Listen to the presentation and complete the notes. Compare your answers with a partner.

SUBWAY
a ¹_____ and successful company with more than 36,000 restaurants in ²_____ countries
Reason: people think the food is healthy   Example: ³_____ and low-fat sandwiches
Reason: restaurants open ⁴_____   Example: until 2.00 in the morning
Reason: food depends on the ⁵_____ and the religion   Example: no beef in sandwiches in ⁶_____

5 Work with a partner. Organize the notes about the company Pizza Hut under the headings.

pizzas are popular all over the world
different kinds of restaurant
Pizza Hut – a large and successful company
pizzas in Germany not the same as pizzas in Thailand
take-away and dine-in restaurants
different pizzas all over the world
it employs 30,000 people and has restaurants in 94 countries

PIZZA HUT	
Main idea:	
Reason 1	Example:
Reason 2	Example:
Reason 3	Example:

6 Work with a partner. Take turns to be Student A and Student B. Follow the instructions. Use the notes in exercise 5.

Student A	Student B
1 Say the main idea. Give a reason.	2 Interrupt and ask for an example.
3 Give an example.	4 Ask Student A to repeat it.
5 Repeat the example and give another reason.	6 Interrupt and say you want to ask a question. Ask a question.
7 Answer the question. Finish your talk.	

9 Astronomy

LISTENING The solar system

1 Work with a partner. Match a word with a definition.

1 ☐ astronomy   a) a small rock or planet that goes round the Sun
2 ☐ the solar system   b) the study of the Sun, Moon, planets, and stars
3 ☐ an asteroid   c) the Sun and the planets that move around the Sun

2 Look at the picture and the title of the lecture.
Work with a partner. Answer the questions.

1 What is the lecture about?
2 How many planets are there?
3 Which planet has rings?

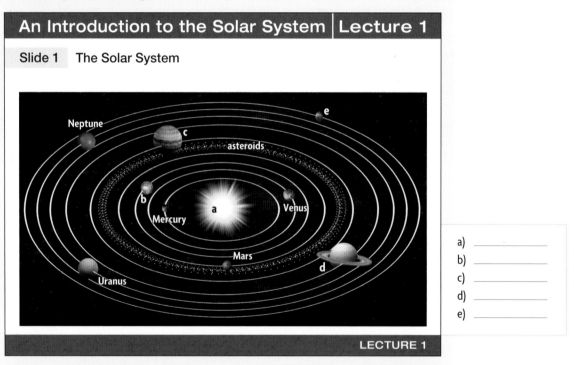

An Introduction to the Solar System | Lecture 1

Slide 1   The Solar System

a) _____
b) _____
c) _____
d) _____
e) _____

LECTURE 1

3 🎧 9.1 Listen to the introduction to the lecture. Number the topics in the order the lecturer is going to talk about them.

☐ asteroids
☐ Mars
☐ the Inner and Outer planets

4 **Read STUDY SKILL** Match an expression with a picture **a** to **f**.

1 at the top
2 on the left
3 in the corner
4 in the centre
5 at the bottom
6 on the right

a ___ b ___ c ___ d ___ e ___ f ___

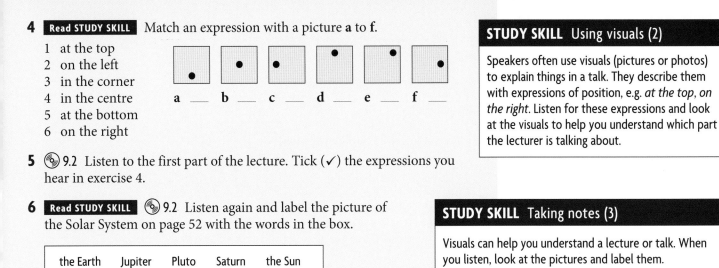

STUDY SKILL Using visuals (2)

Speakers often use visuals (pictures or photos) to explain things in a talk. They describe them with expressions of position, e.g. *at the top, on the right*. Listen for these expressions and look at the visuals to help you understand which part the lecturer is talking about.

5 9.2 Listen to the first part of the lecture. Tick (✓) the expressions you hear in exercise 4.

6 **Read STUDY SKILL** 9.2 Listen again and label the picture of the Solar System on page 52 with the words in the box.

| the Earth | Jupiter | Pluto | Saturn | the Sun |

STUDY SKILL Taking notes (3)

Visuals can help you understand a lecture or talk. When you listen, look at the pictures and label them.

7 9.3 Listen to the second part of the lecture. Label the picture of Mars with the words in the box. Compare your answers with your partner.

An Introduction to the Solar System | Lecture 1

Slide 2 Mars, the red planet

LECTURE 1

craters
ice clouds
north polar ice cap
south polar ice cap
volcanoes

1 _____
2 _____
3 _____
4 _____
5 _____

8 9.3 Listen again and answer the questions. Compare your answers with your partner.

1 How far is Mars from the Sun?
  a) 230 km
  b) 230,000 km
  c) 230,000,000 km
2 What is the diameter of Mars?
  a) 700 km
  b) 7,000 km
  c) 7,000,000 km
3 How high is the mountain on Mars?
  a) 2 km
  b) 12 km
  c) 22 km

KEY LANGUAGE Big numbers

1 Match the numbers with how you say them.

1 ☐ 350,000	a)	thirty-five thousand
2 ☐ 35,000	b)	thirty-five million
3 ☐ 35,000,000	c)	three hundred and fifty thousand

2 🎧 **9.4** Listen and tick (✓) the number you hear. Compare your answers with your partner.

1	a) ☐ 400	b) ☐ 4,000
2	a) ☐ 500	b) ☐ 5,000
3	a) ☐ 8,000	b) ☐ 8,000,000
4	a) ☐ 750	b) ☐ 750,000
5	a) ☐ 4,550,000	b) ☐ 45,500,000

3 **Read STUDY SKILL** Work with a partner. Practise saying the numbers in exercise 2.

STUDY SKILL Saying big numbers

When you say big numbers, add *and* after *hundred*.

350	*three hundred **and** fifty*
5,670 euros	*five thousand, six hundred **and** seventy euros*
8,450,000 km	*eight million, four hundred **and** fifty thousand kilometres*

There is no *s* when we say *hundred*, *thousand*, or *million* in the plural.

two hundred, four thousand, five million

🎧 9.5 Listen.

---

4 🎧 **9.6** Listen and complete the sentences with the numbers.

1 Sound travels at _____ kilometres per hour.
2 Light travels at _____ kilometres per second.
3 The rings of Saturn are over _____ kilometres round.
4 The temperature on the surface of the Sun is about _____ °C.
5 The orbit of the Earth is _____ kilometres.

5 Work with a partner. Student A, look at page 75. Student B, look at page 78.

5,670

11,015

44,000

62,304

9,752,000

SPEAKING Looking at the Moon

1 **Read STUDY SKILL** Complete the description of the phases of the Moon with expressions of position.

"Slide 3 shows the different phases of the Moon. Do you understand 'phase'? A 'phase' is a time, or stage, when something is changing or growing. [1]__In the centre__ of the picture is the Earth. The Moon travels round the Earth in about 30 days, and at each phase, we can see a different part of the Moon. On Day 1 we can't see anything. This is the new Moon [2]_____ of the picture. Are you with me? Then the Moon continues travelling around the Earth, and we see more of it. [3]_____ of the picture in the centre is the first quarter of the Moon, and we can see half of it. Then Day 14 is the full, or whole, Moon [4]_____. After that the Moon gets smaller. [5]_____ of the picture in the centre we can see the last quarter, or half Moon, on Day 21. The last phase, on Day 29.5, is the new Moon again. Is that clear?"

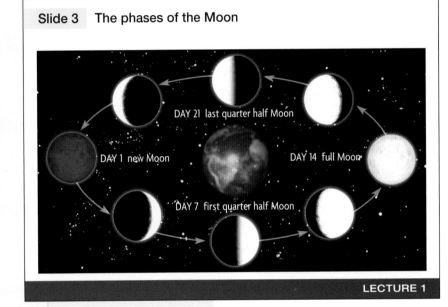

An Introduction to the Solar System | Lecture 1

Slide 3   The phases of the Moon

DAY 21 last quarter half Moon

DAY 1 new Moon

DAY 14 full Moon

DAY 7 first quarter half Moon

LECTURE 1

2 9.7 Listen and check your answers.

3 Work with a partner. Take turns to describe a position of the Moon in the picture in Slide 3. Your partner says the phase of the Moon.

A It's at the bottom, in the centre.
B It's the first quarter half Moon.

4 **Read STUDY SKILL** Underline three checking questions in the lecture in exercise 1.

5 Work with a partner. Student A, look at page 75. Student B, look at page 78.

VOCABULARY DEVELOPMENT
Using visuals to record vocabulary

1 **Read STUDY SKILL** Label the picture of the Earth with the words in the box.

| equator | North Pole | South Pole |

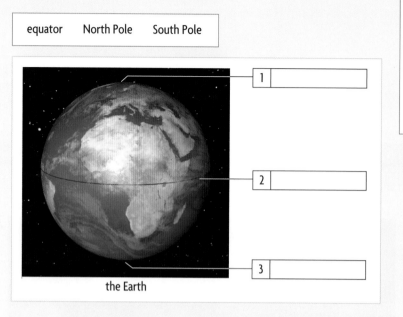

the Earth

1
2
3

STUDY SKILL Recording vocabulary (3)

Use visuals to record new vocabulary in your notebook or a computer file.
- Label pictures.
- Copy pictures from the Internet and write the word under the picture.
- Draw pictures.

Check the word stress in an online dictionary.

2 Use your computer to find pictures for the words in the box. Copy and paste the pictures into your computer file and label them.

| moon | mountain | planet | volcano |

3 Compare your answers with a partner.

4 Draw a picture of a computer in your notebook. Label it with the words in the box. Check the word stress.

| keyboard | memory stick | mouse | screen |

5 Work in pairs. Choose a method to record the words in each topic with pictures.

cars	library	laboratory
bonnet	books	bench
number plate	bookshelves	microscope
wheel	chair	stool
windscreen	desk	test tube

REVIEW

1 Work with a partner. Look at the picture and the title of the lecture. What is the lecture about?

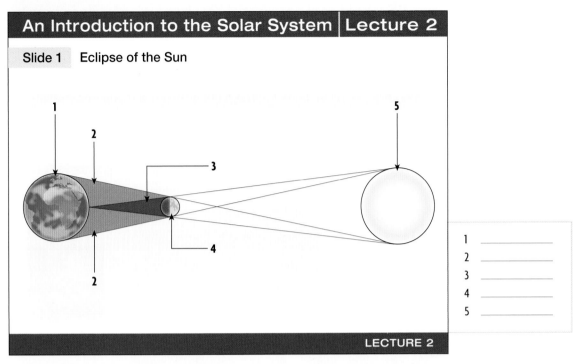

2 🎧 9.8 Listen to the lecture and label the picture with the words in the box.

Earth   Moon   penumbra   Sun   umbra

3 🎧 9.8 Listen again and answer the questions.
1 How far is the Sun from the Earth?
  a) 45,000   b) 145,000 km   c) 145,000,000 km
2 How far is the Moon from the Earth?
  a) 384,000 km   b) 483,000 km   c) 548,000 km
3 How big is the diameter of the umbra?
  a) 130 km   b) 150 km   c) 170 km

4 Write a different big number in each box in Table 1.

Table 1		

Table 2		

5 Work with a partner. Do not look at your partner's book. Take turns to:
- tell your partner your numbers in Table 1.
- check your partner understands you.
- complete Table 2 with your partner's numbers.

The number at the top in the centre is ...

LISTENING SKILLS Intensive listening
SPEAKING SKILLS Preparing a presentation • Giving a presentation (2)
VOCABULARY DEVELOPMENT Recording vocabulary (4) and (5)

LISTENING A role model

1 Work with a partner. Look at the notice. Answer the questions.

1 What do you know about the three people in the pictures?
2 Which job is more important? Why?
3 Do you have any role models? Who? Why?

Role models today

In the third of our talks about role models, the Brazilian architect Maria Soles talks about the person who inspired her career.

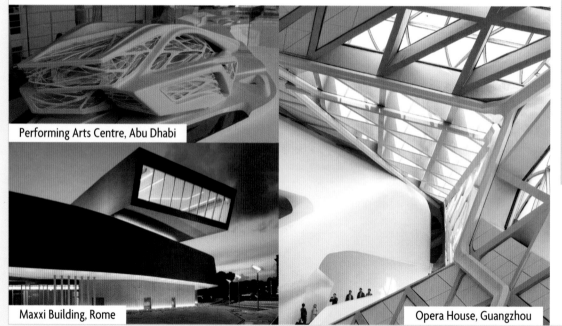

Performing Arts Centre, Abu Dhabi

Maxxi Building, Rome

Opera House, Guangzhou

Steve Jobs
businessman / inventor

Sebastian Vettel
racing driver

Zaha Hadid
architect

2 **Read STUDY SKILLS REVIEW** Look at the notice again. Which person from exercise 1 is the talk about?

3 🔊 10.1 Listen to the introduction to the talk. What is the talk about?

a) Zaha Hadid's buildings
b) her family
c) her life

STUDY SKILLS REVIEW Intensive listening

It is important to prepare before listening intensively. Look back at the Study Skills in the Listening sections of this book. Think about:

- the topic. What do you know about it?
- the title, visuals, and handouts. What is the talk about?
- the introduction. How is the talk organized?
- the information you need. What do you need to listen for?
- taking notes. Is it better to use headings, a diagram, or a timeline?
- using your notes. What do you need to do with your notes, e.g. give a presentation, write an essay?

4 🎧 **10.1** Listen again and look at the notes. Complete headings A and B.

ZAHA HADID		
A Background and _____	B _____	C Successes
born: Baghdad, Iraq in ¹_____	1977: architecture ⁴_____	2002: design competition in Singapore
studied: ²_____ in Beirut	later started a ⁵_____	2004: 1st ⁷_____ to win
architecture in ³_____		Pritzker Prize
	became ⁶_____ for	2010: Stirling Prize for Maxxi building
	Contemporary Arts Center, USA in 2004	in ⁸_____

5 🎧 **10.2** Listen to the talk and complete the notes.

6 Work with a partner. Answer the questions from your notes.

1 When was Zaha Hadid born?
2 What subjects did she study?
3 What was her job in 1977?
4 What did she do after teaching?
5 When did she win the Pritzker Prize?
6 Where is the Maxxi building?

7 Work with a partner. Look at the notice for a careers talk, and the picture. Answer the questions.

1 Where is the talk?
2 Who is the speaker?
3 What is his job?
4 What is the talk about?

8 🎧 **10.3** Work in small groups. Tick (✓) the topics you expect to hear. Listen to the talk and check your answers.

☐ school sports
☐ school studies
☐ university studies
☐ family
☐ learning to fly
☐ interviews

9 Work with a partner. Make questions about Alan with the words.

1 what / study / school
2 what / study / university
3 where / learn to fly
4 why / go on / course
5 when / get / licence

10 🎧 **10.3** Listen again. Make notes using headings or a timeline.

11 Work with a partner. Use your notes to answer the questions in exercise 9.

CAREERS TALK

How to become a pilot

Today's talk is by Captain Alan Naylor, Chief Pilot, United World Airline

in the School Hall
at 3.00 p.m.

SPEAKING   What do you want to do?

1 Match a picture with a word in the box.

| a businesswoman | a doctor | an engineer | a lawyer | a teacher | a vet |

2 Work with a partner. Ask and answer the questions.
1 What did you want to do when you were a child?
2 What do you want to do now?
3 What do you need for this job?

3 ▐ Read STUDY SKILL ▌ Work with a partner. Look at the notes. Which are about a career in law (L)? Which are about a career in medicine (M)?

1 [L] university – law degree 3 years

2 [M] very good school examination results – sciences, e.g. biology

3 [ ] school subjects not important but good examination results

4 [ ] work in a hospital – first training 2 years

5 [ ] 2nd job – work with other lawyers and study – specialist training 1–2 years

6 [ ] university – do a medical degree 5 years

7 [ ] work in a hospital or clinic – specialist/professional training 3–8 years

8 [ ] 1st job – work and study law subject, e.g. business law 1 year

STUDY SKILL   Preparing a presentation

It is important to prepare well before a presentation.
- Choose the topic.
- Do research and get information about the topic.
- Make notes. Use headings, a diagram, or a timeline.
- Organize your notes, e.g. *early life / education / achievements / school / university / after university*.

4 Work with a partner. Student A, organize the notes about a career in law. Student B, organize the notes about a career in medicine. Use headings or timelines.

5 `Read STUDY SKILLS REVIEW` Prepare a short presentation on your topic in exercise 4 on page 60.

STUDY SKILLS REVIEW   Giving a presentation (2)

Look back at the Study Skills in the Speaking sections of this book. When you give a presentation:

- introduce yourself and say what your topic is.
- say how your talk is organized.
- present the main idea. Give reasons and examples.
- speak clearly. Pause at the end of sentences and after each main idea.
- repeat or rephrase important or difficult information.
- look at all your listeners.
- check everyone understands.

Remember to answer any questions politely and thank your listener(s).

6 Work with a partner. Take turns to give your presentation. Look at the list in the Study Skills Review. Tick (✓) the things your partner did.

7 Work in groups of four. Look at page 79. Do the speaking task.

VOCABULARY DEVELOPMENT
Choosing vocabulary to record

1 `Read STUDY SKILL` Add a heading in the box to a group of words.

Opposites	Topic areas	Word families	Words that go together

○ ○ ○ ○ ○ ○ ○ ○ ○ ○ ○ ○ ○ ○ ○ ○ ○ ○ ○ ○

1 _____

do homework

listen to a talk

STUDY SKILL   Recording vocabulary (4)

Think about:

- how to record vocabulary, e.g. words that go together, word families.
- what to record, e.g. word stress, pronunciation, part of speech.

This helps you use new words correctly.

○ ○ ○ ○ ○ ○ ○ ○ ○ ○ ○ ○ ○ ○ ○ ○ ○ ○

2 _____

engine / engineer / engineering

manage / manager / management

○ ○ ○ ○ ○ ○ ○ ○ ○ ○ ○ ○ ○ ○ ○ ○ ○ ○

3 _____

difficult ≠ easy

wet ≠ dry

○ ○ ○ ○ ○ ○ ○ ○ ○ ○ ○ ○ ○ ○ ○ ○

4 _____

study: research / library / classes / degree

space: planets / stars / moons / asteroids

2 Write the correct heading from exercise 1 on page 61 for the groups of words.

1 _____ architecture: buildings / design / plans
2 _____ cold ≠ hot
3 _____ expensive ≠ cheap
4 _____ law / lawyer
5 _____ make notes
6 _____ pilot: fly / navigation / weather
7 _____ read an article
8 _____ teach / teaching / teacher

3 Look at the vocabulary record. Add the missing headings.

| example   irregular forms   meaning   part of speech |
| pronunciation   translation |

word	1 _____	2 _____	3 _____	4 _____	5 _____	6 _____
write	/raɪt/	verb	wrote/written	put letters on paper/screen	Last night, I wrote an email to my brother.	écrire

4 **Read STUDY SKILL** Work with a partner. Write four words in the box under each heading.

| biology   degree   disease   factory   finance |
| hospital   industry   lecture   management |
| microchip   processor   program   software |
| study   timetable   vaccine |

STUDY SKILL Recording vocabulary (5)

You do not need **all** the words you read and hear in English. Choose words that are important in **your** studies and record them in a notebook or computer file.

1 all students	2 medical students	3 business students	4 IT students
_____	biology	_____	_____
_____	_____	_____	_____
_____	_____	_____	_____
_____	_____	_____	_____

5 Choose ten words from the book. Decide how to record them and what to record.

6 Work with a partner. Compare your records. Explain your choices.

REVIEW

1 Work with a partner. Answer the quiz questions with a word from the box.

Arabic
Chinese
English
Persian/Farsi
Portuguese

Language Quiz

What language do people speak in …

1 Brazil? _____
2 New Zealand? _____
3 Morocco? _____
4 Hong Kong? _____
5 Iran? _____

2 10.4 Listen and check your answers.

3 Look at the notice for a talk, and the picture.
What is the talk about?
 a) a career in languages?
 b) a career in sciences?
 c) a career in business?

4 10.5 Listen to the introduction to the presentation
and check your answer.

5 10.5 Listen again. Number the topics 1–3 in the
order you hear them.

 ☐ working as an interpreter
 ☐ the reason for becoming an interpreter
 ☐ subjects to study

6 10.6 Work with a partner. Listen to the presentation.
Student A, make notes about the speaker's early life and
school studies. Student B, make notes about the speaker's
university studies and first job.

7 Work with a partner. Use the words to make questions
about the speaker. Take turns to ask and answer the
questions from your notes.

An international career in communication

A talk by Ms Carrie Evans

at 10.30 on Tuesday 12th January
in the Main Hall

Student A
1 what / study / at university?
2 what / do / after her degree?
3 what / be / first job?
4 where / bank / have / big office?

Student B
1 where / be / from?
2 where / live / as a young child?
3 when / return / England?
4 what / study / at school?

8 Prepare a short presentation about a career.
 1 Research the topic and make notes. For example, for this career, what
  subjects do people study at school / at university?
 2 Organize your notes.
 3 Practise giving the talk.

9 Work in small groups. Take turns to give and listen to the presentations. Take
notes from your partners' presentations. Ask them questions.

AUDIO SCRIPTS

UNIT 1

🔊 1.1

R = Rosa   P = Paul

R Good morning! I'm Rosa, Rosa Cortez from Brazil. What's your name?
P Hello, Rosa. My name's Paul.
R Hi, Paul. Where are you from?
P I'm from Manchester in the UK.
R Ah, Manchester. Like the football club!
P That's right. I'm on a history course. What about you?
R I'm an English student.

🔊 1.2

1 What's your name?
2 How are you?
3 Where are you from?
4 What do you do?
5 What's your degree subject?

🔊 1.3

Conversation 1
R = Receptionist   T = Thomas

R Good morning! What's your name?
T I'm Thomas, Thomas Weber from Germany.
R Could you spell that, please?
T Certainly. Thomas, that's T-H-O-M-A-S, Weber, W-E-B-E-R.
R Thank you. And, what's your degree subject?
T It's history.

Conversation 2
R = Receptionist   T = Turan

R Good morning! What's your name?
T Turan Erdem.
R And where are you from, Turan?
T I'm from Turkey.
R Ah, Turkey! And, what do you do?
T I'm a police officer.

Conversation 3
R = Receptionist   N = Noor

R Welcome to the College. What's your name?
N It's Noor Al Mansoori. I'm from the UAE.
R Ah yes, and what's your degree subject?
N English.
R Sorry, could you repeat that, please?
N English.
R Thank you. And what do you do, Noor?
N I'm a secretary.

🔊 1.4

How do you spell that?

Could you spell that, please?

My name's Thomas, that's T-H-O-M-A-S.

🔊 1.5

The alphabet

a b c d e f g h i j k l m n o p q r s t u v w x y z

🔊 1.6

/eɪ/	say:	a, h, j, k
/iː/	be:	b, c, d, e, g, p, t, v
/e/	egg:	f, l, m, n, s, x, z
/aɪ/	my:	i, y
/əʊ/	no:	o
/uː/	you:	q, u, w
/aː/	car:	r

🔊 1.7

1 a e i o u
2 m t f d s
3 c p t b v
4 j g d k z
5 t v l f n

🔊 1.8

1 What's your name?
2 Where are you from?
3 What course are you on?
4 What do you do?

🔊 1.9

Conversation 1

A What's your name?
B My name's Alan Waters.
A Sorry, could you say that again, please?
B Alan, Alan Waters.

Conversation 2

A Where's Noor from?
B The UAE.
A Sorry?
B The UAE.

🔊 1.10

Good morning!	Good morning!
Good afternoon!	Good afternoon!
Good evening!	Good evening!
Hello!	Hello!
Hi!	Hi!
Goodbye!	Goodbye!
Bye!	Bye!
Nice to meet you.	Nice to meet you, too.
How are you?	Fine, thanks. And you?
See you later.	See you later.
See you tomorrow.	Yes, see you tomorrow.

🔊 1.11

1 Good morning!
2 Nice to meet you!
3 How are you?
4 Good evening!
5 See you later.
6 Goodbye!

1.12

1 Underline the word 'evening'.
2 Match the times and greetings.
3 Circle the letter 'j'.
4 Tick number 12.
5 Complete the sentence with the correct verb.

1.13

I'm sorry, I don't understand.
Could you speak more slowly, please?
What does 'difficult' mean?
How do you say this in English?
What is 'difficult' in Arabic?

1.14

A Good morning.
B Good morning. I want to have some English conversation classes.
A Yes, of course. What's your name?
B I'm Susanne Bertrand.
A Sorry, how do you spell your family name?
B Bertrand. B-E-R-T-R-A-N-D.
A Thank you. And where are you from, Susanne?
B I'm from France.
A France. And what course are you on?
B I'm a business studies student.
A Good. What's your level of English, Susanne?
B I think I'm Intermediate.
A Fine, thank you. Now let's look at the timetable …

UNIT 2

2.1

Let's look at Mexico City. In June, the climate is warm and dry. The temperature during the day is about 25 degrees Celsius. There are about seven hours of sun a day.

2.2

I come from Singapore. In June, the weather is hot and rainy. During the day the temperature is about 31 degrees Celsius. There are about six hours of sun a day.

2.3

Let's look at Mexico City. In June, the climate is warm and dry.

2.4

Good morning, my name is Diana. I come from Malta. My talk is about the weather in my country. In June, it is hot and dry. The temperature is 28 degrees Celsius, and there are about eleven hours of sun a day.

2.5

1 2 3 4 5 6 7 8 9 10
11 12 13 14 15 16 17 18 19 20

2.6

a 5 7 19 20
b 4 11 14 17
c 1 3 6 12
d 2 10 13 18

2.7

a 50
b 90
c 20
d 100
e 60
f 80
g 70
h 30
i 40

2.8

thirteen
thirty
fourteen
forty

2.9

a 40
b 50
c 16
d 70
e 18
f 19

2.10

1 In London in June, the temperature is about 21 degrees Celsius.
2 There are about seven hours of sun a day.
3 The class starts at 10 o'clock.
4 I'm 18 years old.
5 There are 15 students in my class.

2.11

1 Good morning. My name is Roberto and I come from New York. My talk is about my city.
2 Hello, I'm Sally. My city is very nice.

2.12

sunny
important

2.13

1 rainy
2 degree
3 understand
4 Singapore
5 climate
6 eleven

2.14

two syllables	three syllables
complete	adjective
number	afternoon
sixteen	syllable
student	
tourist	
weather	

2.15

1 understand
2 predict
3 morning
4 agriculture
5 eighteen
6 partner
7 thirty

2.16

a Rome is the capital city of Italy. It is a very popular place for tourists.
b Rome is famous for the Coliseum and other very old buildings.
c About ten million tourists visit each year. They come from all around the world. A lot of the tourists visit in May because the weather is very good.

2.17

Good afternoon. My name is Marlu Manlapaz and my talk is about Manila. Manila is the capital city of the Philippines. It is famous for the Malacanang Palace and Rizal Park. About one million tourists visit Manila each year. April is a good month to visit because it is warm and dry, and the temperature is about 34 degrees. There are lots of good hotels and restaurants …

UNIT 3

3.1

1 use a computer
2 watch television
3 travel by bus
4 visit famous places

3.2

I'm a student here in London. In my free time I visit famous places. I travel by bus. I drink coffee with my friends and walk in the parks. In the evenings, I talk to my host family and sometimes I watch television. I also talk to my friends on the Internet and I go on Facebook.

3.3

A = Ahmed   P = Paul

A Hello?
P Hello, Ahmed. It's Paul.
A Hi Paul. How are you?
P I'm fine, but I don't have the new timetable for Mondays. Do you have it?
A Yes, I do. In the morning, at 9 o'clock we have chemistry, and then maths at 11. In the afternoon, at 2 o'clock, there's a biology class.
P OK, so when do we have English?
A It's at 4 in the afternoon.
P That's great. Thank you.
A OK. You're welcome. See you soon.
P Yeah, bye.

3.4

1 eight o'clock
2 eleven fifteen
3 four forty
4 nine thirty
5 six twenty-five
6 one forty-five
7 seven fifty-five
8 two fifty

3.5

Fatima is a business studies student. On Mondays, she has lectures in the mornings. She has lunch at 12.30. In the afternoons, she works in the library. She watches television in the evenings. She sees her friends at weekends.

3.6

A Excuse me, Gina!
B Yes?
A Could I ask you some questions about your study habits, please?
B OK.
A Are you a student here?
B Yes, I am.
A Do you work in the library?
B Yes, I do.
A Do you use the computers here?
B No, I don't.
A Do you do any sport at the university?
B Yes, I do. I play basketball.
A Thank you.
B You're welcome!

3.7

1
A Could I ask a question, please?
B Yes, of course.
A When do we give in the homework?
B On Monday morning.
A Thank you.
2
A Excuse me! Where's Room A5?
B I'm sorry, I don't know.
3
A Thank you for your help.
B You're welcome.

3.8

Sonchai is a student from Thailand. He's on a maths course. He has lectures in the mornings and he uses his computer in the afternoons. In his free time, he plays football with his friends. After football, he drinks coffee with his friends. Sonchai also plays tennis. In the evenings, he watches television and goes on the Internet.

UNIT 4

🎧 4.1

P = Presenter

P Good evening. My guests tonight are Dr Emiko Ikegama and Dr Arjun Mehta, and the subject is oil. Now Dr Ikegama …

🎧 4.2

P = Presenter   I = Dr Ikegama   M = Dr Mehta

P Good evening. My guests tonight are Dr Emiko Ikegama and Dr Arjun Mehta, and the subject is oil. Now, Dr Ikegama, you work on an oil rig in the Gulf of Mexico.

I That's right.

P And Dr Mehta, you work in the oil industry, too, but you work in the desert.

M Yes, I do. Dr Ikegama and I do similar work, but in very different places.

P Dr Ikegama, tell us about your working day.

I Well, we work long hours. We start …

🎧 4.3

I = Dr Ikegama

I Well, we work long hours. We start at 5.30 in the morning and finish about 7.00 in the evening. My main job is to check the weather. The weather is very important at sea. But I also have meetings with the engineers.

🎧 4.4

P = Presenter   I = Dr Ikegama   M = Dr Mehta

P What are the good things and bad things about your work, Dr Mehta?

M Well, I think the long hours are bad because I get very tired.

I I agree! I also think it's difficult working in bad weather.

M That's right, it is. But I enjoy working in the desert because it's very beautiful.

I Also, I miss my family because I only see them four times a year. But I enjoy my work because my colleagues are nice.

🎧 4.5

A I think learning English is important because it is the world language now.

B I agree. I also think it's important because most information on the Internet is in English.

C Sorry, I don't agree. You can find lots of information in other languages, now. But I think English is important because we use it for travelling.

🎧 4.6

A I think computer games are great because they are fun.

B Sorry, I don't agree. I think they're boring.

C That's right. It is better to do a sport or talk to your friends.

B I agree. People spend too much time on the computer.

🎧 4.7

1 speaks writes
2 says uses
3 watches crosses

🎧 4.8

/s/ write writes
/z/ leave leaves
/ɪz/ wash washes

🎧 4.9

/s/ writes helps thinks works
/z/ leaves does goes lives
/ɪz/ washes crosses teaches watches

🎧 4.10

Student A
1 My father goes to work by car.
2 My sister works for an oil company.
3 My aunt teaches at the university.

Student B
1 My mother does art classes.
2 My cousin lives in New York.
3 My brother watches a lot of television.

🎧 4.11

'play' is pronounced /pleɪ/ not /pəleɪ/.
'screen' is pronounced /skriːn/ not /səkriːn/.

🎧 4.12

Group A	Group B	Group C	Group D
please	dry	speak	stress
place	dress	space	strong
plane	drive	spell	street

🎧 4.13

P = Presenter

P Good evening. The subject of tonight's discussion is the advantages and disadvantages of working at home. What do you think, Steven?

🎧 4.14

S = Steven   L = Laura   P = Presenter

S I'm an IT consultant and I work from home. I think working at home is a good thing because I can choose my working time.

L Sorry, Steven, but I don't agree. I think working at home is bad because I don't meet people. I work alone.

P Good point. So, Steven, what other advantages are there to working at home?

S Well, I like working at home because I don't have to travel to work. No buses or trains for me.

L That's true but I still think …

UNIT 5

🎧 5.1

Part 1

Good afternoon everyone. Today's lecture is about braille. Well, what is braille? Braille is a way of reading and writing a language. It is for blind people – people who cannot see. Braille uses dots for letters. Blind people feel and read the dots with their fingers.

There is braille in many languages and there are different ways of writing braille. For example, we usually write Arabic from right to left but in braille we write it from left to right. In Chinese it is very different, because the dots are the sounds of the language, not the letters.

5.2

Part 2

Now, let's look at the dots in braille. They are in two columns, or lines, of three. Slide 1 shows the places for the dots. As you can see, the letter 'a' has one dot in the first column. The letter 'b' has two dots and the letter 'c' has a dot in both columns. The letter 'x' has four dots. There are 63 possible positions for the dots.

Braille also has signs for punctuation. Slide 2 shows some of these signs. As you can see, there is a sign for a capital letter. This comes before the letter.

5.3

1 Good afternoon. My name is Akemi. My talk today is about body language.
2 Hi. I'm Yoshi. Body language is important.

5.4

Good afternoon. My name is Akemi. My talk today is about body language. This is when people use their eyes and their hands to give more information. We all use body language when we speak, for example, in presentations or discussions. Body language is different in different cultures, for example …

5.5

listen   watch

5.6

answer lamb light business half hour friend

5.7

Good morning. Today's lecture is about hand signals. What are hand signals for? Well, they are a way of giving instructions using your hands and arms. The police use them to control the traffic and tell drivers what to do.

Slide 1 shows a hand signal which means stop. The police officer holds their right arm up, with the palm facing the traffic. The second slide also shows a signal for stop. This is for traffic coming from behind the police officer. Slide 3 shows the sign that means go. The officer holds their right arm up. The back of the hand faces the traffic. The officer moves their hand towards their face. This shows the drivers they can now go.

UNIT 6

6.1

Introduction

Good morning. The seminar today is about the number that we call 'pi'. Firstly, we're going to look at what pi is. Secondly, I'm going to talk about why it is called pi. Then we are going to look at the history of pi. And finally, I am going to look at the uses of this very long number.

6.2

Firstly, what is pi? Well, pi is a useful number because it helps us make calculations about circles. Pi is the circumference of a circle divided by the diameter. It is approximately 3.14. This number is true for all circles.

And why is it called pi? A British mathematician, William Jones, called it pi because pi is the first letter of the Greek word which means 'circumference'.

Now, what is the history of pi? The Egyptians first used pi about 4,000 years ago to build their pyramids. Then in the 3rd century BCE the Greek mathematician, Archimedes, calculated pi to 3 digits. 500 years later, the Chinese mathematician, Liu Hui, calculated pi to 3.141, that's 4 digits. Today, because of computers, we can calculate it to 2.7 trillion digits and more.

And finally, what do we use pi for? Well, we calculate all kinds of things in maths, science, and engineering with pi. It is a very important calculation. For example, in maths we use pi to …

6.3

Firstly, / what is pi? / Well, / pi is a useful number / because it helps us make calculations about circles. / Pi is the circumference of a circle / divided by the diameter. / It is approximately 3.14. / This number is true for all circles. /

And why is it called pi? / A British mathematician, / William Jones, / called it pi / because pi is the first letter / of the Greek word which means 'circumference'.

6.4

Introduction

Good morning. / My lecture today / is about famous mathematicians. / Firstly, / I'm going to discuss the work of Isaac Newton. / Secondly, / I'm going to talk about Albert Einstein. / And finally, / we're going to look at Pythagoras / and how his work influences modern maths today.

6.5

Good afternoon. / My talk today is about maths in different jobs. / Firstly, / I'm going to talk about maths in engineering. / Secondly, / I'm going to look at maths in architecture, / and then / I'm going to discuss how we use it in medicine. / Finally, / I'm going to explain how we use maths in business.

6.6

The Egyptians first used pi / about 4,000 years ago / to build their pyramids.

6.7

study a study a student
invent an invention an inventor
work work a worker
use a use a user
write writing a writer
lecture a lecture a lecturer

6.8

1 My brother teaches at a university. He's a lecturer in economics.
2 I use a computer to write my essays.
3 Many people worked on the invention of the Internet.
4 I would like to study law at university.

6.9

Introduction

Good afternoon. / My talk today / is about the importance / of studying in higher education. / Firstly, / I'm going to look at / what higher education is. / Secondly, / I'm going to talk about / courses and qualifications. / And finally, / I'm going to give you the reasons / for studying in higher education.

6.10

So, firstly, what is higher education? Well, it's education at a college or university after secondary school.

Secondly, what courses can you do and what qualifications do you get at these colleges and universities? A course is usually in only one or two subjects, for example business, or mathematics and computer science. Most students study for a degree or diploma for three or more years, but some students do a one-year foundation programme first.

And finally, people study in higher education for different reasons. Some students want to study because they like a subject and want to learn about it. Other people study a subject because they need it for a job, for example, medicine to be a doctor. And of course, students often get a better job and earn more money if they have a diploma or degree.

UNIT 7

7.1

Good morning and welcome. Today's programme is about the history of the smartphone. We're going to look at four famous companies, and discuss what they developed, and when. So firstly, …

7.2

Good morning and welcome. Today's programme is about the history of the smartphone. We're going to look at four famous companies, and discuss what they developed, and when. So firstly, IBM. IBM produced the 'Simon' in 1992. This was a phone with a calendar, address book, and notepad. You could also use it to send emails. But it only had 1MB of memory and it weighed one pound two ounces, that is, about half a kilogram.

Four years later, in 1996, Nokia made the Nokia 9000. This was a phone and a PDA, that is, a Personal Digital Assistant. It had 8MB of memory. Applications, or apps, used 4MB, programs used 2, and there were 2MB for personal data, in other words, personal information.

Next, Ericsson produced the E380, and they used the word 'smartphone' for the first time. This was in the year 2000. The E380 was a phone, a PDA, and used a touchscreen and keyboard. It was also a new design.

Then, in 2007, the next big step was the Apple iPhone. As I'm sure you know, the iPhone is a lot more than a mobile phone. Today there are more than 500,000 apps for these phones, and …

7.3

1 This was a phone and a PDA, that is, a Personal Digital Assistant.
2 Applications, or apps, used 4MB.
3 There were 2MB for personal data, in other words, personal information.

7.4

At first, television was monochrome, in other words, black and white, and in 1936, there were only 200 televisions in the world. But TV quickly became popular, and by 1950, there were more than ten million worldwide, that is, around the world. Colour TV was the next important development. In 1954, RCA produced its first colour television. It cost $1000. Today this is about eight and a half thousand dollars – very expensive. The first flat screen TVs appeared in the 1960s. There was also a design for plasma televisions in the 1960s but they only took off, or became successful, in the 1990s.

7.5

1 nineteen thirty-eight
2 seventeen oh five
3 twenty twenty
4 two thousand

7.6

1 twenty fourteen
2 eighteen sixty-seven
3 seventeen oh seven
4 sixteen thirty-two
5 nineteen sixteen

7.7

the first of January
the nineteenth of March
the twenty-second of August

7.8

My talk is about the history of telecommunications, that is, communications using radio, phones, and the computer. Firstly, Alexander Graham Bell …

7.9

discovered
started
crossed

7.10

/d/ live lived
/ɪd/ want wanted   decide decided
/t/ watch watched

7.11

/d/ appeared called organized tried
/ɪd/ added invented
/t/ helped liked looked

7.12

1 web page
2 word processor
3 address book
4 memory stick
5 computer chip

7.13

1 keyboard
2 headphones
3 home page
4 laptop
5 touchscreen
6 computer game

7.14

Today's programme is about the seventh generation of video game consoles. We're going to discuss important developments by three famous companies: Microsoft, Sony, and Nintendo.

7.15

Today's programme is about the seventh generation of video game consoles. We're going to discuss important developments by three famous companies: Microsoft, Sony, and Nintendo.

The seventh generation, in other words, the seventh important development, of game consoles began on 22nd November 2005, in the USA. Microsoft produced the Xbox 360. This has a hard drive and is very fast. You can also play DVD games and movies on it.

Then, in Japan, Sony produced PlayStation 3 on 11th November 2006. This machine also has a hard drive and can play Blu-ray disk games and movies.

Only about one week later, on 19th November 2006, Nintendo started selling the Nintendo Wii in North America. This new console is compatible, that is, can work with, old Nintendo games.

What the next generation, the eighth …

7.16

The seventh generation, in other words, the seventh important development, of game consoles began on 22nd November 2005, in the USA.

This new console is compatible, that is, can work with, old Nintendo games.

UNIT 8

8.1

Introduction

A Good afternoon, everyone. Today I'm going to discuss the size of the car industry worldwide. As you probably all know, the car industry is very large. The industry is large in three ways: the number of vehicles it produces, the number of people working in the industry, and also the amount of money it makes.

8.2

Part 1

A The car industry is a large industry, firstly, because many people in the world want to have a car and secondly, because now more people can buy a car. The industry now produces 78 million vehicles a year and this is going to grow as the world population increases and more people want their own car. When an industry is this big, of course, it needs a huge number of employees. About 150 million people work in the industry around the world. That's a lot of people! And it makes a large amount of money. It is now worth about 700 billion dollars a year.

8.3

Part 2

A Right, next I'm going to talk about how international the car industry is. It is very international because today car companies make and sell cars in many countries worldwide. 50 countries in the world now produce cars.
B Excuse me, could you repeat that number, please?
A Yes, 50, five oh, countries in the world. Some of these countries, such as Chile, make about five thousand vehicles a year, but in other countries, it's many more. For example, China produces millions of vehicles.
B There are many different types of vehicles.
A Yes, by vehicles, I mean cars, lorries, and buses. China is now the number one producer. It produces more cars than any other country. But the Japanese car manufacturer Toyota is very successful. It has factories in 27 countries.
C Excuse me, could I ask you a question? Why is Toyota so successful?
A There are three reasons for that. Firstly, because it makes small, cheap cars, such as the Yaris. Secondly, it makes good quality cars, for example, there are very few mechanical problems. And finally, it's successful because it thinks about the future and what the next development in cars is.
C Sorry, could you give me an example of that?
A Yes, of course – hybrid and electric cars.

8.4

There are many parts to the clothing industry. I am going to talk about one part: designer labels, for example, Gucci, Prada, and Ralph Lauren. These companies make a lot of products, such as clothes, handbags, and jewellery. Designer labels are very popular because they use good quality materials and the products are fashionable. But they can be quite expensive. For example, a pair of Armani jeans can cost nearly 500 euros.

8.5

1 A These companies make a lot of products.
   B Excuse me, could I ask a question? What do they make?
2 A Designer labels are very popular because they use good quality materials.
   B Sorry, could you give me an example of the materials?
3 A A pair of Armani jeans can cost nearly 500 euros.
   B Could you repeat the price, please?

8.6

Introduction

A Good afternoon. Today I'm going to talk about the fast food company Subway. Subway is a very large and successful business today and I'm going to explain the reasons for its success.

8.7

A Good afternoon. Today I'm going to talk about the fast food company Subway. Subway is a very large and successful business today and I'm going to explain the reasons for its success. So, how large is Subway? Well, it has more than 36,000 restaurants in 98 countries.
B Excuse me, could you repeat the numbers, please?
A Yes, more than 36,000 restaurants in 98 countries. And it's successful because people think that the food, such as salads and low-fat sandwiches, is healthy. Secondly, Subway is successful because it opens late, for example, until 2.00 in the

morning in some places. Also, the food in the sandwiches depends on the country and the religion.

C Sorry, could you give me an example?

A Yes, in India the sandwiches don't have beef in them …

UNIT 9

🔊 9.1

Introduction

Good afternoon. In this lecture I'm going to give you a short introduction to the solar system. Firstly, we're going to look at the Inner and Outer planets, then we're going to talk about Mars, and finally we're going to discuss asteroids.

🔊 9.2

Part 1

So, let's start with the planets. My first slide shows the solar system. As you can see, there are nine planets. In the centre of the picture you can see the Sun. The Inner planets are nearest the Sun, and these are Mercury, Venus, the Earth, and Mars. You can see the Earth on the left of the picture. To give you an idea of distance, it's about 150 million kilometres from the Sun. Then there are five Outer planets – Jupiter, on the left at the top, and Saturn at the bottom on the right, with its rings. Do you understand 'rings'? They are circles around the planet. Then there's Uranus, Neptune, and Pluto. Pluto is at the top of the picture, on the right. Between the Inner and Outer planets there are asteroids. I'm going to talk about these in a minute.

🔊 9.3

Part 2

So now we are going to look at the planet Mars, also known as the red planet. Mars is about 230,000 km from the Sun and is smaller than the Earth. Its diameter is about 7,000 km. Slide 2 is a picture of Mars. On the right at the top there are two black areas. These are craters. On the left of the craters there are volcanoes. Mars has a lot of volcanoes and mountains. Interestingly, the highest mountain in the solar system is on Mars, and it's 22 km high. At the top of the picture is the north polar ice cap and at the bottom is the south polar ice cap. On the left of the south polar ice cap there are ice clouds made of carbon dioxide.

Now, moving on to talk about asteroids …

🔊 9.4

1 4,000
2 500
3 8,000
4 750,000
5 45,500,000

🔊 9.5

three hundred and fifty
five thousand, six hundred and seventy euros
eight million, four hundred and fifty thousand kilometres
two hundred   four thousand   five million

🔊 9.6

1 Sound travels at 1,225 kilometres per hour.
2 Light travels at 299,792 kilometres per second.
3 The rings of Saturn are over 3 million kilometres round.
4 The temperature on the surface of the Sun is about 5,500° Celsius.
5 The orbit of the Earth is 940 million kilometres.

🔊 9.7

Slide 3 shows the different phases of the Moon. Do you understand 'phase'? A 'phase' is a time, or stage, when something is changing or growing. In the centre of the picture is the Earth. The Moon travels round the Earth in about 30 days, and at each phase, we can see a different part of the Moon. On Day 1 we can't see anything. This is the new Moon on the left of the picture. Are you with me? Then the Moon continues travelling around the Earth, and we see more of it. At the bottom of the picture in the centre is the first quarter of the Moon, and we can see half of it. Then Day 14 is the full, or whole, Moon on the right. After that the Moon gets smaller. At the top of the picture in the centre we can see the last quarter, or half Moon, on Day 21. The last phase, on Day 29.5, is the new Moon again. Is that clear?

🔊 9.8

A Good morning. Today I'm going to talk about an eclipse of the Sun. Firstly, I'm going to talk about how this happens, and then we're going to see when and where the next eclipses are going to be.

So, my first slide shows an eclipse of the Sun. As you can see, the Sun is on the right and the Earth is on the left. On the right of the Earth, in the centre, is the Moon. Now, the Sun is 145 million kilometres from the Earth, and the Moon is only 384 thousand kilometres from the Earth. Is that clear?

B Could you repeat those numbers, please?

A Yes, the Sun is 145 million kilometres from the Earth and the Moon is 384 thousand kilometres away. Of course, the Sun is much bigger than the Moon, but because the Sun is far away, the Sun and the Moon look the same size in the sky. Are you with me? When the Moon passes in front of the Sun, it blocks, or stops, the light from the Sun. It makes a shadow on the Earth. The shadow is in two parts. In the centre is the umbra. Do you understand 'umbra'? It is another word for shadow. The umbra is a very small area, about 150 km in diameter. This is where it is very dark. The other parts, at the top and at the bottom of the umbra on the slide, are called the penumbra. This area is in part shadow, so only partly dark. An eclipse only lasts for a few minutes as the Moon moves around in the sky …

UNIT 10

🔊 10.1

Introduction

Good morning! My name's Maria Soles and I am an architect. I am here today to tell you about the life of a person I admire: the architect Zaha Hadid. When I learnt about her, I wanted to be an architect, too. So, first I'm going to tell you about her background and education, then about her career, and finally, about some of her great successes.

10.2

Good morning! My name's Maria Soles and I am an architect. I am here today to tell you about the life of a person I admire: the architect Zaha Hadid. When I learnt about her, I wanted to be an architect, too. So, first I'm going to tell you about her background and education, then about her career, and finally, about some of her great successes.

Zaha Hadid was born in Baghdad, Iraq in 1950. She studied maths at university in Beirut and graduated in 1971. Then, in 1972, she went to London to study architecture.

She began her career as an architecture teacher in 1977, and later started a business. She designed lots of buildings but she didn't build many of them. Then, in 2004, she designed the Contemporary Arts Center in Cincinnati in the USA and became world-famous.

She has many successes. In 2002, she won the international design competition in Singapore. In 2004, she was the first woman to win the Pritzker Architecture Prize. Then, in 2010, she won the Stirling Prize for the Maxxi building in Rome. Today, she is …

10.3

Good afternoon, everybody. My name is Alan Naylor. I'm very happy to be back at my old school. The head teacher asked me to tell you about how to become a pilot. So, I'm going to tell you how I became interested in flying, the studies I did, and about my career after university.

When I was a child, I loved planes. I watched them in the sky and I knew I wanted to be a pilot.

At school I studied maths and physics because you need these subjects to be a pilot. Then I went to university to study engineering. I also joined a flying club and learnt to fly.

In my last semester at university, I wrote to lots of airlines and applied for a job. I thought it was easy! But there were more things I needed to do. So, I went on a course, because I wanted to get my airline pilot's licence. I learnt about the weather, and navigation, and lots of other things.

Finally, I got my licence in 1980, and went for an interview with an international airline. I passed the interview and got the job, but I still had a lot to learn, and I'm still learning!

10.4

1 People in Brazil speak Portuguese.
2 People in New Zealand speak English.
3 People in Morocco speak Arabic.
4 People in Hong Kong speak Chinese.
5 People in Iran speak Persian, or Farsi.

10.5

Introduction

Good morning, everyone. I am here to tell you about a career in interpreting, that is, translating words from one language into another language. Firstly, I'm going to tell you why I became an interpreter. Then I'm going to talk about the studies I did, and finally, about having an international career as an interpreter.

10.6

I am English, but when I was a young child my parents lived in Tokyo. So, I learnt to speak Japanese with my friends at school. I loved speaking two languages and I wanted to learn more. When I was 15, we returned to England and I went to secondary school. I studied English, Japanese, and Spanish.

Then I went to university and studied International Law and Japanese. When I finished my degree, I stayed at university and did a one-year diploma in interpreting. After all my studies, my first job was with an international bank. The bank had a big office in Japan. I helped the bank understand their Japanese customers. I interpreted the words from Japanese into English. It was very hard work but I enjoyed it …

PAIRWORK

Student A Unit 1 Key language ex 4 (p6)

1 Say and spell your words.

  1 bag
  2 dictionary
  3 desk
  4 pen
  5 board

2 Listen to your partner. Write the words you hear.

  1 _____
  2 _____
  3 _____
  4 _____
  5 _____

Student A Unit 1 Speaking ex 4 (p7)

1 Look at the badges. Ask your partner questions. Complete Badge 1.

What's your name?

Ask your partner to repeat or spell difficult words.

COLLEGE OF FURTHER STUDIES   **Badge 1**

WELCOME DAY

NAME _____
COUNTRY _____
DEGREE SUBJECT _____
OCCUPATION _____

2 Answer your partner's questions about Badge 2. Repeat or spell difficult words.

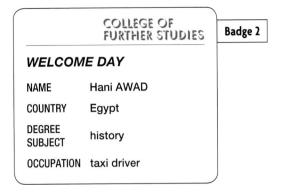

COLLEGE OF FURTHER STUDIES   **Badge 2**

WELCOME DAY

NAME	Hani AWAD
COUNTRY	Egypt
DEGREE SUBJECT	history
OCCUPATION	taxi driver

Student A Unit 2 Key language ex 6 (p12)

1 Make the sentences true for you.

  1 I am _____ years old.
  2 I have _____ brother(s).
  3 I have _____ sister(s).
  4 _____ people live in my house.
  5 I watch _____ hours of television a week.

2 Read your sentences to your partner.

3 Listen and complete the sentences about your partner.

  1 My partner is _____ years old.
  2 She / He has _____ brother(s).
  3 She / He has _____ sister(s).
  4 _____ people live in my partner's house.
  5 She / He watches _____ hours of television a week.

Student A Unit 2 Speaking ex 6 (p13)

1 Prepare a talk using the information in CITY FILE 4.

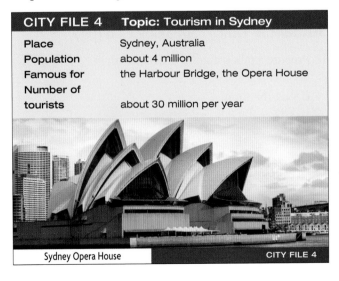

CITY FILE 4	Topic: Tourism in Sydney
Place	Sydney, Australia
Population	about 4 million
Famous for	the Harbour Bridge, the Opera House
Number of tourists	about 30 million per year

Sydney Opera House   CITY FILE 4

2 Give your talk.

3 Listen to your partner's talk. Complete CITY FILE 5.

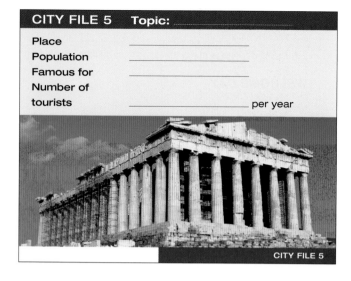

CITY FILE 5	Topic: _____
Place	_____
Population	_____
Famous for	_____
Number of tourists	_____ per year

CITY FILE 5

Student A Unit 3 Key language ex 4 (p17)

1 Look at the timetable. Ask Student B what time lectures are on Monday. Write the times.

When is the English lecture on Monday?

Lectures	Monday	Tuesday
English		9.45
biology		11.20
chemistry		1.50
maths		4.10

2 Answer Student B's questions about lecture times on Tuesday.

Student A Unit 5 Speaking ex 8 (p31)

1 Complete the information.

> Good _____ . My name is _____
> _____ . My talk today is
> _____ sign language. Sign language is for
> people who cannot hear. It uses hands, arms, and
> expressions to communicate. Sometimes sign
> language is not the same as spoken language. For
> example, in the USA and Britain the spoken language
> is the same but the sign language is very different.

2 Practise giving the talk. Read the talk aloud.

3 Give your talk to your partner.

4 Listen to your partner give their talk. Tick (✓) the boxes about your partner's talk.

	Very good	Good	OK
Speaking clearly	☐	☐	☐
Body language	☐	☐	☐
Pauses	☐	☐	☐

Student A Unit 7 Key language ex 5 (p42)

1 Ask your partner the questions. Write the answers.

1 When is your birthday?	_____
2 What is the date today?	_____
3 What year did you start school?	_____
4 What is the last day of the year?	_____
5 What is an important date for you? Why?	_____

2 Answer your partner's questions.

Student A Unit 7 Speaking ex 8 (p43)

1 Prepare a talk using the information in the table.

- Say the topic.
- Order the talk.
- Explain the underlined words.
- Practise the talk.

Topic – Developments in digital cameras		
Who	What	When
Logitech	sold 1st commercial digital camera	1990
Casio	produced 1st digital camera with LCD	1995
Sharp	made 1st commercial mobile phone with digital camera	2000

commercial = something that people can buy
LCD = a screen (liquid crystal display) used on mobile phones and digital watches

2 Give your talk to your partner.

3 Listen to your partner's talk. Complete the information in the timeline.

Topic – Four important IT companies			
1_____ made computer 2_____	IBM produced 1st 3_____	Steve Jobs, Steve Wozniak started 4_____	Michael Dell started Dell
1968	1975	1976	5_____

Student A Unit 8 Speaking ex 10 (p49)

1 You are going to give a talk about Rolex watches. Organize the notes about Rolex watches under the headings.

ROLEX WATCHES	
They are expensive.	Rolex watches are very famous.
They work very well.	They always give the right time.
They last a long time.	GMT Masters II costs 8,000 euros.
They can last 60 years.	

Main idea:	
Reason 1	Example:
Reason 2	Example:
Reason 3	Example:

2 Give your talk to your partner.

3 Listen to your partner's talk. Complete the notes. Ask questions to check your understanding.

Main idea:	
Reason 1	Example:
Reason 2	Example:
Reason 3	Example:

Student A Unit 9 Key language ex 5 (p54)

1 Ask Student B the questions. Read out answers a), b), and c). The correct answer is underlined.

1 What is the temperature on Venus?
   a) 465° Celsius *four hundred and sixty-five degrees Celsius*
   b) 45° Celsius
   c) 4° Celsius

2 How many Earth years does it take Pluto to go round the Earth?
   a) 24
   b) 248
   c) 2,480

3 How far is Jupiter from Earth?
   a) 58 million km
   b) 588 million km
   c) 5,880 million km

4 How many moons does Saturn have?
   a) 2
   b) 6
   c) 62

5 How hot is the centre of the Earth?
   a) 75° Celsius
   b) 750° Celsius
   c) 7,500° Celsius

2 Listen to Student B's questions. Choose a), b), or c).

Student A Unit 9 Speaking ex 5 (p55)

1 Read the text about telescopes.

> A telescope is a long round object. We use telescopes to see things that are very far away because they make these things look bigger. This is very useful for looking at the planets and stars. There are different kinds of telescope. The reflector telescope is very popular.

2 Your partner has the same picture of a reflector telescope, but with different information. Describe the labels on your picture to your partner. Check your partner understands.

The telescope has different parts. On the right is ...

3 Listen to your partner describe their picture. Complete the labels on your picture.

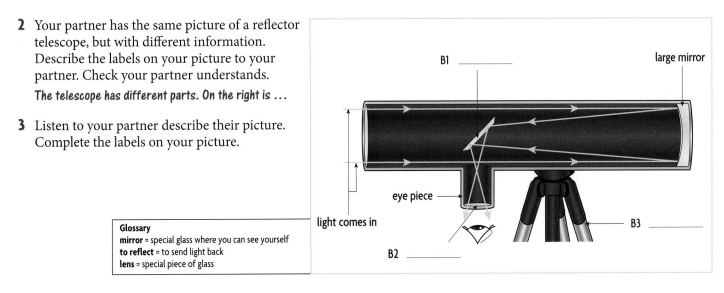

Glossary
mirror = special glass where you can see yourself
to reflect = to send light back
lens = special piece of glass

B1   large mirror

eye piece

light comes in

B2   B3

Student B Unit 1 Key language ex 4 (p6)

1 Listen to your partner. Write the words you hear.

1 _____
2 _____
3 _____
4 _____
5 _____

2 Say and spell your words.

1 laptop
2 phone
3 keys
4 paper
5 money

Student B Unit 1 Speaking ex 4 (p7)

1 Look at the badges. Answer your partner's questions about Badge 1. Repeat or spell difficult words.

> **COLLEGE OF FURTHER STUDIES** | Badge 1 |
>
> *WELCOME DAY*
>
> NAME   Anne BERMANN
> COUNTRY   Switzerland
> DEGREE SUBJECT   mathematics
> OCCUPATION   shop assistant

2 Ask your partner questions. Complete Badge 2.

What's your name?

Ask your partner to repeat or spell difficult words.

> **COLLEGE OF FURTHER STUDIES** | Badge 2 |
>
> *WELCOME DAY*
>
> NAME   _____
> COUNTRY   _____
> DEGREE SUBJECT   _____
> OCCUPATION   _____

Student B Unit 2 Key language ex 6 (p12)

1 Make the sentences true for you.

1 I am _____ years old.
2 I have _____ brother(s).
3 I have _____ sister(s).
4 _____ people live in my house.
5 I watch _____ hours of television a week.

2 Listen and complete the sentences about your partner.

1 My partner is _____ years old.
2 She / He has _____ brother(s).
3 She / He has _____ sister(s).
4 _____ people live in my partner's house.
5 She / He watches _____ hours of television a week.

3 Read your sentences to your partner.

Student B Unit 2 Speaking ex 6 (p13)

1 Prepare a talk using the information in CITY FILE 5.

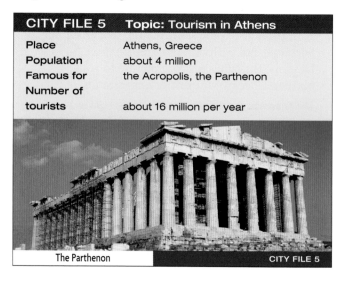

CITY FILE 5	Topic: Tourism in Athens
Place	Athens, Greece
Population	about 4 million
Famous for	the Acropolis, the Parthenon
Number of tourists	about 16 million per year

The Parthenon   CITY FILE 5

2 Listen to your partner's talk. Complete CITY FILE 4.

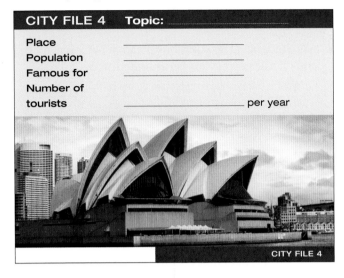

CITY FILE 4 Topic: _____

Place _____
Population _____
Famous for _____
Number of
tourists _____ per year

CITY FILE 4

3 Give your talk.

Student B Unit 3 Key language ex 4 (p17)

1 Look at the timetable. Answer Student A's questions about lecture times on Monday.

Lectures	Monday	Tuesday
English	9.15	
biology	10.35	
chemistry	2.25	
maths	4.40	

2 Ask Student B what time lectures are on Tuesday. Write the times.

When is the English lecture on Tuesday?

Student B Unit 5 Speaking ex 8 (p31)

1 Complete the information.

Good _____ . My name is _____
_____ . My talk today is
_____ Morse code. Morse code is an
international form of communication. It uses light or
sounds to communicate letters. People in ships use
Morse code when they cannot communicate by radio
or phone. It is very useful in an emergency.

2 Practise giving the talk. Read the talk aloud.

3 Listen to your partner give their talk. Tick (✓) the boxes about your partner's talk.

	Very good	Good	OK
Speaking clearly	☐	☐	☐
Body language	☐	☐	☐
Pauses	☐	☐	☐

4 Give your talk to your partner.

Student B Unit 7 Key language ex 5 (p42)

1 Answer your partner's questions.

2 Ask your partner the questions. Write the answers.

1 What year were you born in?	_____
2 What was the date yesterday?	_____
3 When did you start learning English?	_____
4 What is the first day of the year?	_____
5 What is an important date for you? Why?	_____

Student B Unit 7 Speaking ex 8 (p43)

1 Prepare a talk using the information in the timeline.
- Say the topic.
- Order the talk.
- Explain the underlined words.
- Practise the talk.

Topic – Four important IT companies

Intel made computer <u>chips</u>	IBM produced 1st <u>personal computer</u>	Steve Jobs, Steve Wozniak started Apple	Michael Dell started Dell
1968	1975	1976	1984

chips = very small things for computer memory
personal computer = a computer for one person to use, not businesses or colleges

2 Listen to your partner's talk. Complete the information in the table.

Topic – Developments in digital [1]_____

Who	What	When
Logitech	[2]_____ 1st commercial digital camera	1990
Casio	produced 1st digital camera with [3]_____	1995
Sharp	made 1st commercial [4]_____ with digital camera	[5]_____

3 Give your talk to your partner.

Student B Unit 8 Speaking ex 10 (49)

1 You are going to give a talk about Gucci. Organize the notes about Gucci under the headings.

GUCCI
It sells clothes, jewellery, sunglasses, and handbags.
Gucci is successful all over the world.
Famous people often like its products.
Its products are good quality and expensive.
It makes many products.
Some football players wear Gucci clothes.
A handbag can cost thousands of dollars.

Main idea:	
Reason 1	Example:
Reason 2	Example:
Reason 3	Example:

2 Listen to your partner's talk. Complete the notes. Ask questions to check your understanding.

Main idea:	
Reason 1	Example:
Reason 2	Example:
Reason 3	Example:

3 Give your talk to your partner.

Student B Unit 9 Key language ex 5 (p54)

1 Listen to Student A's questions. Choose a), b), or c).

2 Ask Student A the questions. Read out answers a), b), and c). The correct answer is underlined.

1 What is the average temperature on the Earth?
   a) <u>7° Celsius</u> *seven degrees Celsius*
   b) 17° Celsius
   c) 27° Celsius
2 How many Earth days is a day on Venus?
   a) 2
   b) 24
   c) <u>243</u>
3 How old is the Earth?
   a) <u>more than 5 billion years old</u>
   b) more than 50 billion years old
   c) more than 500 billion years old
4 What is the maximum speed of the wind on Neptune?
   a) 21 km per hour
   b) 210 km per hour
   c) <u>2,100 km per hour</u>
5 How hot is the surface of the Sun?
   a) 500° Celsius
   b) <u>5,500° Celsius</u>
   c) 55,000° Celsius

Student B Unit 9 Speaking ex 5 (p55)

1 Read the text about telescopes.

> A telescope is a long round object. We use telescopes to see things that are very far away because they make these things look bigger. This is very useful for looking at the planets and stars. There are different kinds of telescope. The reflector telescope is very popular.

2 Your partner has the same picture of a reflector telescope, but with different information. Listen to your partner describe their picture. Complete the labels on your picture.

3 Describe the labels on your picture to your partner. Check your partner understands.

The telescope has different parts. In the centre is …

Glossary
mirror = special glass where you can see yourself
to reflect = to send light back
lens = special piece of glass

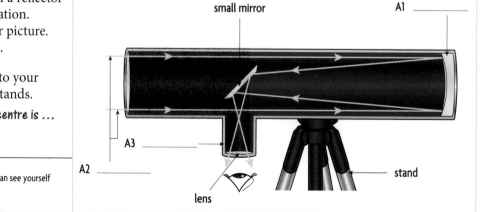

Speaking task Unit 10 Speaking ex 7 (p61)

1 Choose a topic from your own studies, for example, an important person, an invention, a discovery.

2 Research your topic and make notes.

3 Organize your notes for a two-minute talk. See Study Skills Review p61 to help you.

4 Plan the introduction. Include:
- a greeting.
- the topic.
- the organization of the talk.

5 Decide which words and expressions to rephrase or explain.

6 Practise your talk. Think about stressing important words and pausing after main ideas and at the end of sentences.

8 In your group, take turns to give and listen to the presentations. Take notes from the presentations.

9 Compare your notes with a partner.

PHONETIC SYMBOLS

Consonants

1	/p/	as in	**pen**	/pen/
2	/b/	as in	**big**	/bɪg/
3	/t/	as in	**tea**	/tiː/
4	/d/	as in	**do**	/duː/
5	/k/	as in	**cat**	/kæt/
6	/g/	as in	**go**	/gəʊ/
7	/f/	as in	**four**	/fɔː/
8	/v/	as in	**very**	/ˈveri/
9	/s/	as in	**son**	/sʌn/
10	/z/	as in	**zoo**	/zuː/
11	/l/	as in	**live**	/lɪv/
12	/m/	as in	**my**	/maɪ/
13	/n/	as in	**near**	/nɪə/
14	/h/	as in	**happy**	/ˈhæpi/
15	/r/	as in	**red**	/red/
16	/j/	as in	**yes**	/jes/
17	/w/	as in	**want**	/wɒnt/
18	/θ/	as in	**thanks**	/θæŋks/
19	/ð/	as in	**the**	/ðə/
20	/ʃ/	as in	**she**	/ʃiː/
21	/ʒ/	as in	**television**	/ˈtelɪvɪʒn/
22	/tʃ/	as in	**child**	/tʃaɪld/
23	/dʒ/	as in	**German**	/ˈdʒɜːmən/
24	/ŋ/	as in	**English**	/ˈɪŋglɪʃ/

Vowels

25	/iː/	as in	**see**	/siː/
26	/ɪ/	as in	**his**	/hɪz/
27	/i/	as in	**twenty**	/ˈtwenti/
28	/e/	as in	**ten**	/ten/
29	/æ/	as in	**stamp**	/stæmp/
30	/ɑː/	as in	**father**	/ˈfɑːðə/
31	/ɒ/	as in	**hot**	/hɒt/
32	/ɔː/	as in	**morning**	/ˈmɔːnɪŋ/
33	/ʊ/	as in	**football**	/ˈfʊtbɔːl/
34	/uː/	as in	**you**	/juː/
35	/ʌ/	as in	**sun**	/sʌn/
36	/ɜː/	as in	**learn**	/lɜːn/
37	/ə/	as in	**letter**	/ˈletə/

Diphthongs (two vowels together)

38	/eɪ/	as in	**name**	/neɪm/
39	/əʊ/	as in	**no**	/nəʊ/
40	/aɪ/	as in	**my**	/maɪ/
41	/aʊ/	as in	**how**	/haʊ/
42	/ɔɪ/	as in	**boy**	/bɔɪ/
43	/ɪə/	as in	**hear**	/hɪə/
44	/eə/	as in	**where**	/weə/
45	/ʊə/	as in	**tour**	/tʊə/

OXFORD
UNIVERSITY PRESS

Great Clarendon Street, Oxford, OX2 6DP, United Kingdom

Oxford University Press is a department of the University of Oxford.
It furthers the University's objective of excellence in research, scholarship,
and education by publishing worldwide. Oxford is a registered trade
mark of Oxford University Press in the UK and in certain other countries

ISBN: 978 0 19 474169 9

Printed in China

This book is printed on paper from certified and well-managed sources

ACKNOWLEDGEMENTS

Illustrations by: Kathy Baxendale pp.17, 57, 73, 75, 76, 78; Mark Duffin pp.33,
40 (IBM Simon), 40 (Nokia 9000), 52, 55, 56; Melvyn Evans pp.10, 21

*We would also like to thank the following for permission to reproduce the following
photographs:* Alamy pp.4 (university buildings/Justin Kase zsixz), 4 (library/
Claudia Wiens), 5 (moodboard), 9 (FancyVeerSet7/Fancy), 11 (Singapore/
GoPlaces), 12 (birthday card/Stuart Miles), 13 (Statue of Liberty/Michal Besser),
15 (Rizal Park/Ivan Nesterov), 15 (Grand Palace/Friedrich Stark), 16 (2/Kevin
Foy), 16 (4/David Jones), 18 (2/Jandke/Caro), 18 (3/Leandro Mise), 19 (lunch/
Datacraft - Sozaijiten), 37 (Radius Images), 39 (Ulrich Baumgarten/vario
images GmbH & Co.KG), 41 (Braun TV/INTERFOTO), 45 (Xbox/Gavin Rodgers),
46 (blue hatchback/Paul Rapson), 46 (Seminar 1 centre/A ROOM WITH
VIEWS), 46 (Seminar 1 right/Transtock Inc.), 46 (Seminar 1 left/My Story),
48 (Dolce & Gabbana/EmmePi Travel), 48 (Prada/EAP EAP), 48 (Gucci/M.Flynn),
48 (DKNY/Maurice Savage), 51 (sandwich/Foodcollection.com), 51 (burger/
amphotos), 58 (Sebastian Vettel/citypix), 58 (Opera House/Hufton + Crow/
VIEW Pictures Ltd), 58 (Maxxi Building/Luke Hayes/VIEW Pictures Ltd), 60 (6/
Mike Abrahams); Corbis pp.7 (teacher and student/Alex Mares-Manton/Asia
Images), 15 (Malacanang Palace/Paul Almasy/Historical), 18 (1/Tim Pannell/
Flame), 22 (desert oil well/Joho/cultura), 22 (Indian engineer/Hugh Sitton/Flirt),
27 (man at desk/Matthias Ritzmann/Blink), 35 (Pythagoras/Gianni Dagli Orti/
Fine Art), 43 (Jason Szenes/Corbis Wire); ESA p.53 (ESA/MPS for OSIRIS Team,
PS/UPD/LAM/IAA/RSSD/INTA/UPM/DASP/IDA); Getty Images pp.7 (students/
Echo/Cultura), 15 (Coliseum/Buena Vista Images/Photodisc), 16 (1/zhang bo/
the Agency Collection), 18 (4/Jamie Grill/Iconica), 19 (squash/Tobias Titz),
22 (oil rig/Harald Sund/Photographer's Choice), 22 (female engineer/BJI),
23 (desert storm/by Philippe Reichert/Flickr), 23 (storm at sea/Arnulf Husmo/
Stone), 24 (tutorial/Don Bayley/the Agency Collection), 24 (gamer/Vincent
Ricardel/The Image Bank), 27 (woman/Tim Robberts/The Image Bank),
28 (Hill Street Studios/Workbook Stock), 29 (Billy Hustace), 30 (man blue
tie/Wavebreakmedia Ltd/the Agency Collection), 30 (woman speaking/Ron
Krisel), 35 (Newton/Sir Godfrey Kneller/The Bridgeman Art Library), 36 (maths
equation/Jeffrey Coolidge/The Image Bank), 41 (flatscreen TV/Yasuhide
Fumoto/Digital Vision), 43 (Library of Congress/Science Faction), 43 (Library
of Congress/Science Faction), 43 (Noah Seelam/AFP), 45 (PlayStation/
Holloway/Stone), 45 (Wii/altrendo images/Stockbyte), 49 (Karim Sahib/AFP),
58 (Zaha Hadid/Al Bello/Getty Images Sport), 59 (Rob Melnychuk/Photodisc),
61 (Purestock), 63 (hana/Datacraft); iStockphoto pp.6 (drink/new), 6 (car/
Henrik Jonsson), 10 (andres balcazar), 12 (clock/VisualField), 12 (thermometer/
rzelich), 17 (new), 21 (darren wise), 22 (radio presenter/sturti), 30 (man blue
top/Tadej Zupancic), 30 (young girl/paul kline), 40 (smartphone/Roberto A
Sanchez), 44 (headphones/pagadesign), 44 (keyboard/new), 44 (laptop/David
Vernon), 46 (white van/TommL), 46 (bus/Tupungato), 58 (Steve Jobs/GYI NSEA),
60 (2/kristian sekulic), 60 (3/kristian sekulic), 73 & 77 (travellinglight); Rex
Features pp.35 (Einstein/Courtesy Everett Collection), 47 (View China Photo),
58 (performing arts centre/Tony Kyriacou); Royalty-free pp.13 (Empire State
Building/image100), 16 (3/Martin Dalton), 60 (1/White), 60 (4/Photodisc), 60 (5/
Fancy), 74 & 76 (Photodisc); Science & Society Picture Library p.41 (Marconi
TV/NMPFT Photo Studio); Shutterstock pp.6 (phone/Sergej Razvodovskij),
6 (salad/Dmitry Melnikov), 11 (Malta/new), 15 (floating markets/Juriah Mosin),
34 (Evgeny Murtola), 36 (tennis/new), 36 (sales graph/new), 46 (lorry/Adrian
Reynolds), 50 (new2), 51 (pizza/new2)